The Trinity

Carl Puylaert

Preface   9

Part 1: The Three Powers   14

1.   It started with capital.   16

1.1.   Definition of capital   16
1.1.1.   Available capital.   17
1.1.2.   Working capital.   18
1.1.3.   Used capital.   20

1.2.   The self evidence of capital.   21
1.2.1.   Using in harmony.   22

1.3.   The separation of capital and organisation   23
1.3.1.   The growth of the company.   25
1.3.2.   Corporate raider the reason for the decline of the 80's.
          26
1.3.3.   The suspicious shareholder.   28
1.3.4.   Debts and credits not based on capital.   29

1.4.   Capital as way to equalise

1.1.   By needs   32
1.1.1.   By process.   33
1.1.2.   By market.   33

1.2.   Capital subordinate to the trinity   34
1.2.1.   Capital subordinate to labor.   34
1.2.2.   Capital subordinate to nature.   35

2.   Organising labor.   37

2.1.   Coming together   38
2.2.   By groups of mutual interests.   38
2.2.1.   By democratic vote.   39
2.2.2.   By force.   40

3.   Problems to face   41
3.1.1.   Awareness of the problem.   42
3.1.2.   Existing class system.   43
3.1.3.   No existing infrastructure.   45
3.1.4.   Internal differences.   47

3.2.   Equal representation   48
3.2.1.   The dominance of capital.   49
3.2.2.   The lack of nature.   51
3.2.3.   The impossibility of the equilibrium.   51

3.3.   The controlling task of labor   52
3.3.1.   Together with the government.   54
3.4.   Inside the organisation.   55

4.   Who represents nature.   56

4.1.   What is nature   57
4.1.1.   Earth, water and air.   58
4.1.2.   The animals and greenery.   59
4.1.3.   Nature in today's world.   61
4.1.4.   The trinity as saviour.   63

4.2.   Who will defend nature   64
4.2.1.   The people who defended capital.   65
4.2.2.   The people who defended labor.   65
4.2.3.   Nature itself will accomplish.   66
4.2.4.   The trinity as fourth unit will defend.   67

4.3.   How long before the world will see   68
4.3.1.   More disasters.   69
4.3.2.   What do we need as proof.   70

4.3.3.   Is nature noticeable for the people.   72

4.4.   The future of nature in the society   72
4.4.1.   The future of nature in the corporation.   74
4.4.2.   Nature as possible goal for the religions.   75
4.4.3.   Nature as political party.   76
5.   The future of nature in between people.   77

Part 2: The Solution

6.   The economic vision.

6.1.   The transition
6.1.1.   The future of small businesses.
6.1.2.   The future of big businesses.
6.1.3.   The future of multinationals.

6.2.   The use of existing infrastructure
6.2.1.   Within the business organisation.
6.2.2.   Within the governmental organisation.
6.2.3.   Within the labor organisation.
6.2.4.   Within the religious organisation.
6.2.5.   Within the environmental organisation.

6.3.   Transitional problems
6.3.1.   Transition of budgets.
6.3.2.   Transition of technology.
6.3.3.   Transition of communication and transportation.

6.4.   Price forming
6.4.1.   Reducing the capital's share.
6.4.2.   Limiting the labor's share.
6.4.3.   Enlarging natures share.

6.5.   Valuation of the factor nature
6.5.1.   The real impact on society will only result in nominal
          figures.
6.5.2.   The real reason of capital appraisal is the non appraisal of
          nature.

6.5.3.   Valuation by profit possibility, according to the market mechanism.

6.5.4.   The difference between increase and change.

6.6.   The plea for the trinity theories

6.6.1.   The employment of the trinity profit theories.

6.6.2.   Based on the market instead of the production.

6.6.3.   The mathematical model.

6.6.4.   The changes for the total money demand.

6.6.5.   The changes for the international capital goods market.

6.6.6.   The indirect advantage for the developing world in the short run.

7.   The strategic goals and instruments.

7.1.   The instruments of the trinity

7.1.1.   In forming phase.

7.1.2.   By democratic majority.

7.1.3.   With the initial help from economical communities.

7.1.4.   The trinity to force a market price upon nature.

7.1.5.   The transition of force into the equilibrium.

7.2.   The diminishing importance of the government

7.2.1.   Government as a common organisation.

7.2.2.   Companies as a more responsible organisation.

7.3.   All governments as equals

7.3.1.   The unimportance of international debts and credits.

7.3.2.   The unimportance of history.

7.4.   The internationalising

7.4.1.   Advantages for the environment.

7.4.2.   Governments organise their international capital.

7.4.3.   Governments become international.

7.5.   The former trinity as example

7.5.1.   The justice department.

7.5.2.   The people's representatives.

7.5.3.   The government itself.

7.6.   The importance of the government

7.6.1.   Changing of measuring importance.

7.6.2.   Nature as a power to measure the government.

7.6.3.   The developing world becomes equal.

7.7.   Consequences of trinity theories for the government
7.7.1.   The superfluity of environment taxes.
7.7.2.   Minor changes for countries who had environment taxes.
7.7.3.   Regulating the enlarging value of nature.

8.   Quality and quantity results by changing priorities.

8.1.   The proof of the need to change
8.1.1.   Natural disasters.
8.1.2.   Rapidly changing environment.

8.2.   Earth comes in
8.2.1.   World capital flows will diminish.
8.2.2.   Mankind will reduce.

8.3.   Transportation will diminish
8.3.1.   In speed and use transportation will diminish.
8.3.2.   Transportations of men, resources, goods will diminish.
8.3.3.   Communication will take over.

8.4.   Developed against developing
8.4.1.   Quality against quantity.
8.4.2.   Capital against earth and men.
8.4.3.   Honest division of intellect.

8.5.   The need of certain goods
8.5.1.   What is the essence of these goods.
8.5.2.   What are the resources needed.
8.5.3.   What is the consequence to human freedom.

8.6.   Will nature allow us to go back
8.6.1.   Will the trees start growing again.
8.6.2.   Will the ozone layer keep protecting us.
8.6.3.   What will be the advantage for nature to come back.

8.7.   Consequences for nature of trinity theories
8.7.1.   What exactly is a profit to nature.
8.7.2.   Who as intellectual person can judge for nature.
8.7.3.   The two kinds of nature, the one who servers mankind and the one who was and always be.

8.7.4.   Establishing markets for nature shares.
8.7.5.   Capitalist with large natural holdings will become rich by being naturalists.

8.8.   Quantity results of the trinity theories
8.8.1.   The difference in between ex ante and ex post.
8.8.2.   The cost of the factor of production.
8.8.3.   The profit of the factor of production.
8.8.4.   The impossibility of real growth.
8.8.5.   The quantity impact of replacing taxes.
8.8.6.   Equal productivity of the three factors of production.
8.8.7.   The impact on national income.
8.8.8.   The impact on the total money demand and savings.
8.8.9.   The bigger impact on the foreign relations.
8.8.10.   The increase in nature investments.
8.8.11.   The decrease in capital investments.
8.8.12.   The changing consumption out of availability and understanding.

Part 3: Practical

9.   A model of the organisation.

9.1.   Differences in the objective and the way
9.1.1.   The earth as objective.
9.1.2.   Capital as objective.
9.1.3.   Men as objective.

9.2.   How to employ the profit in the right way
9.2.1.   What kind of capital has to diminish.
9.2.2.   What kind of nature has to grow.
9.2.3.   Is labor interfering in the equal profit allocation.

9.3.   The sizes of the organisation
9.3.1.   Down to earth organisations for developing countries.
9.3.2.   Huge organisations for the developed countries.

9.4.   The organisational units
9.4.1.   The goal for the future.
9.4.2.   The board of direction.
9.4.3.   The choice and need of the product.
9.4.4.   The choice of capital.
9.4.5.   The choice of labor.
9.4.6.   The role of nature in the organisation.

10.   The immediate action.

10.1.   In the governmental organisations
10.1.1.   How to reach them.
10.1.2.   How long will it take.

10.2.   In the capital organisations
10.2.1.   How to reach them.
10.2.2.   How long will it take.

10.3.   In the non profit organisations
10.3.1.   How to reach them.
10.3.2.   How long will it take.
10.3.3.   Are controlling organisations still needed

Preface

This is the start of a thesis, which will look into what was, is and can be, if we want to live into a world which will continue the way we know it. It is written out of a certain ideology, where it is believed that capital is becoming a too big a part of the world.
It is not believed that capital in itself is wrong, but because of the overpopulation capital has to be reduced per capita.
After the summit in Rio, June 1992, where the world leaders came together, we know only one thing for sure. The whole world is convinced, we have to start respect the earth by protecting it. Now the world leaders are back home fighting each, their own political problems. And again they have forgotten the question NATURE.
Nature is not visible enough. We need an additional way to bring the solution. A solution, which will not force people to respect nature, but a solution which will show the people that nature deserves respect.
With this thesis, I do not pretend to bring any radical news. But I certainly hope people will take the time to give my view, which I call a sensible solution, on the environmental problems a fair chance.

It is an economical thesis, which is only partly going into the economic structures or economic processes. The study tries to find a manner in which the economic order can be installed in such a way, that the three factors of production will have, each an equal chance to survive. As a result of the changing in the economic order, of course the economic structures and economic processes will adapt. It will have consequences for the macro economical essences, but not to a point that major adaptations need to be made to comprehend the process and structure of the economy.

If we look into the economic history we will see that the economic order this study will present is only a logic follow up.
After the Keynesian changes on the neoclassical theories, it is time that the people start to acquaint with an even more regulated society. At first it was the factor labor which was the motive to adapt the neoclassical theory, now it will be the factor nature, which will be the motive for the adaptations of the Keynesian model. To relate these models to the factors of production is easy to understand if we see the more and more populated world in the context of production. And the total production we see as the total income. The neoclassic, Adam

Smith, saw capital as a lonely factor of production. Keynes brought in government regulations to ensure labor, and after the first half of the twentieth century these two factors of production were the essences of the economy. By now everybody has understood, but not acted on, the fact that nature has to be brought in the model and in the society. Maybe it can be a start of a post industrial model, which can show a possibility how the decision forming will ensure nature of its proper place. The study has not overseen the Post-Keynes, Monetary, Institutional or even Marx theories, because I do not see any saviour for nature from their models either. Nevertheless this study only includes the economic order, and does not pretend anything else as bringing people closer to what has to come.

Part 1 of the thesis handles the three production powers as they are known in the economic science. Capital, Labor and Nature. This thesis reproaches capital of using the science of economics, to prove their existence, but leaving out the two other powers. Here three examples out the reality.

Practical,
1. *It does not make sense that all the board members of direction are representatives of capital.*
2. *It does not make sense that the written objectives of all corporations are the growth and continuation of capital by profit.*
3. *It does not make sense that the organisations only have to carry their responsibility to capital.*

It is the three and not only one power of production which are essential for the continuation of the world. This thesis will try to prove that only with an equal representation of capital, labor and nature in every organisation, the world will have a possibility to survive.
The time has come that the balance between the three powers of production will be adjusted to equality. The natural harmony of capital, labor and nature.

Many economists will argue that the objectives of the corporations are not capital, but profit. Profit as they see it is a reward on the three factors of production. In this case the thesis argues that since the profit is applied for more than one third, the capital part, for the employment of capital itself, it is as a result more rewarding to capital than either labor or nature. The first trinity theory is based upon this:

The rewarding profit on labor, capital and nature, is only rewarding for the factor of production for which the profit is employed.

In reality the profit goes directly into the purchases of capital goods, indirectly in the purchases of consumer goods and into savings which are employed to invest in capital. If we would estimate that eighty percent goes back into capital it would not be overestimated. According to the above theory this would mean that nature and labor are under rewarded.

Part 2 talks about the actual solution. This according to me is a sensible solution, I call the trinity. The trinity should bring capital, labor and nature together. It should be the trinity which will control each independent organisation. I discuss first the organisation itself. Then I go over in the governmental organisations and compare these with the corporate organisations. The solution is a sensible one, because it recognises capital, labor and nature in an equal manner. This is accomplished by giving each person three different vote. One vote for capital representation, one vote for labor representation and one vote for nature representation. It is a democratic solution, which in a way forces people to see all three powers. From these chosen representatives will result equal representations in every organisation.

The only sensible solution, is the form of organisation in which capital, labor and nature are represented in an equal manner, this form I call the TRINITY.

Governmental, religious, capitalistic, labor or environmental organisations all will be represented by the three powers and not by one. The solution lies in the reality that we do not work from above or against any power. The solution works from within. People within the organisation will represent nature and labor as well as capital. It will be impossible for the organisation to go around a power, which forms their own existence. That is why, I call the three powers, the factors of existence. Not only the existence of life, but also the existence of the organisation which is a cell of life, in which nature, capital and labor are all equally represented.

The real problem for the instalment of the trinity is the fact that until now nature is not countable. The people until now never needed to bring nature in the picture. It is for the possibility to count nature that this thesis has deduced a theory.

To grow is a necessity in a world were the population still grows. Profit can be seen as a factor of growth. Even if all available powers grow, w can speak of real growth, because it is not a physical growth of production. It is a growth towards the needs of the growing population. Or an alteration of physics towards the human needs. It is this profit this reward, seen as feedback, which will bring the possibility to count nature. The second theory of the trinity is based on this:

Given the facts that the market will bring a fair price to the used factors of production, and that this market price will be based on the possibility of profit, it is an equal profit which can bring an equal price to the factors of production.

Going with the above theory we only have to divide the reward or profit into an equal share for nature, capital and labor. In doing so we cannot use former quantities. Every profit made by any organisation needs to be divided in three equal parts. In a continuing economic process this profit will set a market price on until this moment unknown nature values. When nature has a profit it will have a value, determined by a market. Also a result will be that since the profit for capital and in a lesser sense for labor will diminish, their market values will diminish. This all however can only take place if the economic order will allow the trinity to divide the profit. Only if the values of nature, capital and labor equally will appear in equal money units, only then nature, capital and labor will equally be recognised.

Where Marshall told in "The Principles of Economics" in 1890, that "accumulation of capital was the power of the growth of prosperity". It was Marx, who told in " Das Kapital" of the theory of the value of labor, "a good has only the value of the needed hours to produce it". It is now time that nature is valued, not by the process of production, like capital and labor, but by the feedback which the consumption is bringing nature by the way of profit. And this time the mistake will not be made that the importance of one factor will diminish the other factors. Because all three will be measured by profit given by the consumer. The consumer will vote for the trinity.

Part 3 is the practical effect of the solution. I did not think my thesis would give any credibility if it would not talk about the actual interpretation of it in real life. To prove this I make a model organisation, in which the trinity is the ultimate responsible. In addition I compare the many different possible organisations and how these will react on the balanced representation of powers. At last I mention an immediate action, which can be brought into reality.

The reason of giving my time to this thesis finds itself in an absolute belief of the injustice of capitalism in our present world. Myself, I was for a long time a convinced capitalist. Very few were as capitalistic oriented as I have practiced ten years of my live. In a way, I feel some guilt, but I do not know if guilt is a good motive. However it gives me inspiration and the will to work. My solution works from the inside of the organisation and not from above or against. It is absolutely not the intention of this study to go against capital or even labor, the study wants capital to participate on an equal level. The balance and the trinity will bring the solution to the liveability of the world as we are familiar with. If we are not going to give recognition to the factor nature, the world will alter in a not human way. We can of course ask if we could live in an altered world, but no human would offer herself of himself as the first victim. This fact should show every human being, that a solution has to come. Sustainable growth is only a goals, now we have to find the way. Maybe the economic science has brought it to us so many years ago. The equal representation of the three powers of production, capital, labor and nature.

en the only visible solution.

Part 1   The Three Powers

The science, economy, studies the behaviour of people. That part of the behaviour which studies the obtaining of goods, for which as little as possible goods should be exchanged, in order to satisfy as much as possible needs. To produce these goods three essential factors are needed.

These three factors are: *1. Capital*
                                 2. Labor
                                 3. Nature

It are these factors of production which will form the essence of this thesis. These factors of production will be called factors of existence or powers of life. People have always divided the earth, according to the person or group interests they have found themselves a way to divide. This thesis is an economical thesis and therefore divides the earth in capital, nature and labor. Everything, tangible or intangible, is under this division a clear part of one of the above powers. As with all divisions, even without human interference, there is an will always be a power struggle to enhance the part it (or one) belongs. As a human behaviour study, economy, looks upon the production as a manner to enlarge human comfort. The existing system at this moment sees the enlargement of the factor capital as the main possibility to enlarge human comfort itself. It is on this front this thesis wants to make an adjustment. It is not only the enlargement of capital, bur the enlargement or profit of the three factors of production which will in the end ensure human comfort.

The today's production apparatus is as follows divided:

According to the economy, nature is;
1. resources,
2. greenery,
3. Natural energy,
4. the earth itself.

Labor is;
1. spiritual,
2. physical.

Capital is;
1. goods to consume,
2. goods to produce,
3. money.

For economic purposes these three factors of production have to be mixed in such a way that the result is the highest growth of the factor capital. The growth is called profit on the production apparatus. But this thesis posits that since profit is employed for the biggest part for capital, it as a result for the biggest part a profit to capital alone. So this is the contradiction I find in the economy. First the economists conclude there are three powers of production. Second the economists conclude only one of these powers we will let grow. Of course there is an explanation for this behaviour. And until now the growth of the population made it necessary to grow the factor capital. For Nature was always there in an abundance. Labor was growing as a simple result of the growth of the population. So the only factor which had to grow was Capital. And therefore the profit was employed for capital and in lesser degrees to the other two factors of production.

As a result we are faced with the contradiction where every single corporation, government and even foundation sees itself forced to bring these three powers together in order to profit only one power, instead of profiting the three powers.

This contradiction I hope, I will be able to denounce, and the result will give the solution. This solution will be a economic democratic order under the form of the trinity. This trinity should bring an even more regulated society. However based upon a market mechanism. The part where the trinity should come in is the profit allocation. The trinity, the thesis, posits if the profit is allocated in an equal manner, nature, capital and labor can be valued in an equal manner.
The main problem we face today, the valuation of the factor nature will also be solved. The neo classics brought a profit allocation which was based only capital. Marx brought a profit allocation which was based only on labor. The trinity will make no such mistake as excluding essential parts and allocate the profit on the trinity itself.

This all is to be understood only possible if it is the choice of human kind to continue the earth as we are familiar with it. It will bring a more regulated, equal and possibly dull society. But the alternative will bring disaster and death and therefore also more excitement.

1.   Definition of capital

Capital refers to all the man made means of production, such as machinery, factories, office buildings, transportation and communications but also the education and training of the labor force. All these in order to enhance the ability to produce. Personally I add to this definition of capital, that all man's creations are a form of capital. All materials, constructed by man, direct of indirect used to produce are a form of capital. So in addition to capital as a factor of production I see capital as a factor of human existence.

The essence of the difference I make is that capital, man and nature are not subordinate to the unit of production. They are subordinate to the trinity itself. The trinity of nature, men and capital. The trinity, which I later call the organisation. The organisation subordinate to the trinity. Not the organisation subordinate to the production of capital.

Under different studies, capital is either one of the factors of production, in which case, labor and earth are the other factors. In other studies, it means that nature is included in the capital factor. What means that there are only two factors, men and nature. In which nature represents all materials. My definition is placed in between the two major definitions.

I see man as one power. Nature as the second power, but I divide Nature in the unmovable and the movable. Where the unmovable is nature and the movable is capital.

This brings us closer to the first definition of nature, capital and men. But, capital includes all man's creations and not only the means of production.

Men, apart from becoming more, basically stay the same. Men are the movers of the capital, which once was nature. Nature is everything left untouched. Capital, however I see as materials, men take and use temporarily from Nature. Capital is given back to nature in a different substance. Capital is thus a man's creation. It is this creation of men, which became in itself more important than men. By now it its of such importance that nature itself is in the process of adjusting to this man's creation. In doing so the earth changes from a hospitable to a more hostile place were men is living. So what always was, the earth an unmovable is now changing, the earth is adjusting. This should learn us to adjust our creations to the earth. Men again is in the position to change, but by now, the movable into the unmovable instead of the unmovable into the movable.

Recognising I do, as powers, factors of production, factors of change, or factors of existence;

1. *Nature, as an unmovable, as the earth itself.*
2. *Men, as movers of movable nature, the accelerating factor.*
3. *Capital, as movable nature, as a man's creation.*

The three I call the trinity, which I call the organisation.

1. Available capital.

The actual availability of capital is unlimited in quantity, since it is possible to reuse. However the reaction of the earth will be so hostile that the simple act of winning capital will become impossible. To give back used movable to the unmovable will not be without retaliation. If the earth is what was, and what was, is good. If men is the accelerator of change. Then capital, what has become bad. This statement based on the fact that the earth is deteriorating. The earth is reacting in a man unkind way on men's creations.

The available capital is the earth itself, the unspoiled, unmoved, untouched earth. But also the already used capital. This we call the possibility of recycling. Recycling capital, which as we can see now is slowing the process of deterioration. If this assumption is based on truth, we can not be sure of. It is very well possible, that reusing capital, and with it separating different materials, has an even worse affect on the earth. There is no way of knowing, since only time can tell.

When men became it was the capital which differentiated him from animals. His ability to move the earth and use it to his advantage was what made him the accelerator. It was such self evidence that there was never any reason to question. Since only mankind could change its destiny and as such had little resistance in growing ahead of other animals. It was history by itself which cleared the path to the present. to use capital in order to enhance men's presence, was never an act against nature. It was always within limits of the greatness of the earth. By now however the capital factor has outgrown men as well as nature.

We, men confront huge masses of available capital, still nature, our reaction is natural, we think it is available to us. This, though, is a mistake. It is not visible to us if this apparent availability is available to us or available to the earth itself. Now the earth is letting us know that the usage will be its own. We have used enough. However at this moment and for the next 50 years we will not be able to stop. Available or not available we have no choice. No choice, because we are loyal to mankind. Not only to mankind, but especially to capital itself. If it would be true that the current problems were a result of loyalty to mankind, problems were explicable. However current problems are a result of loyalty to capital, a man's creation, a creation which is an unnatural part of harmony.

2.   Working capital.

Whatever it is we have taken from the earth, and adjusted for our usage is working capital. We have seen that the availability of capital is basically the earth itself, but only as long as the earth allow us to take. By now the earth is opposing and if we men do not change in the way we handle the earth, it will become more hostile. Working capital, is the state of capital in between the moment of withdrawal from the earth and giving back to the earth. This we call used capital or waste.

In men's eyes used capital is worse as available capital, therefore we call it wasted. In order to be in harmony with most assumptions about capital and the rest of this study, we assume that this indeed is a truth. Going farther on this statement that used capital is waste. We have to conclude that the way we use capital has also influence on the amount of used capital. This because it is possible to recycle or reuse capital. Never the less we can only talk about the quantity, since quality has no value.

No value has quality, because the holds of quality are not known in the timeless earth. Only the vastness of quantity has relevance in the history of the earth, because in the interest of the earth there is no difference in quality.

Timeless, of course, since the existence of the earth has no direct connection with the existence of mankind. in short we do not know if chemical waste or paper waste is of a worse nature to earth in a million years. We do not know if separated waste is of a worse nature than not separated waste. With the present knowledge we have no influence over quality, only over quantity.

The impact on the quality of the earth is not known for two reasons:
1.We are simply not capable of knowing what the earth will become,
2.We are not capable in going back on the process.
However the impact of the quantity is known because of;
1. How many times we recycle,
2. How much we use.

As stated before it goes about the quantity and not the quality.

The consumption, working capitals is the worst capital there is. Capital in itself is worse than men or earth, which makes the available, used and working capital it is also the working capital which is the worst. We talk about the worst for the factor nature. The next assumption I make is that to do something, to create something or to produce something is the worst you can do. And as a direct result the worst which could happen to the world right now is that the developing world will start as ordered by the developed world paying its debt back. In order to do this, the developing world needs to start working. This work will bring so much additional need of capital and additional used capital, that disaster will strike immediately.

Looking to this problem in the Western world, and on a personal level, it is also clear that every single man should work as less as possible. Our whole way of life we should denounce. Every single assumption mankind in the developed world has made is based on the opposite of the welfare of the earth. On the other hand it is of course so that our being in itself is based on activity. Without the activity we would not be. The solution will have to be found from within and there is no reason to believe that this will be impossible.

The earth has allowed us to start and it will allow us to continue. But not based on the one factor of existence, capital. But based on man, earth and capital, the trinity as the one and only. The trinity, which will has its power for endurance, because of a regained harmony.

1.1.3 Used capital.

When men are finished with the gained capital they do not really know what to do with the waste, which I call used capital. As mentioned before, on the long run, I is not necessarily bad to give this waste back in a different form to the earth. But in starting to look for answers we have to look for temporary solutions. This because the other option, the long run, has no answers to us and leaves us doing nothing.

About waste a lot is written and a lot is known. We know that it pollutes our air, our water and our land. Our, because it is a temporary problem. The reactions the earth gives us is directed immediately towards us. It tells us we have reached the limit. We have ways to measure, we have ways to punish pollution. However we do not always know who to blame, since it remains question if the producer of dirt (used capital) or the consumer of goods (working capital) is the one who needs to pay. Of course these ways of human deception are to keep solutions out of reach. It is not the problem inside which frontiers the earth is abused, it is a problem of mankind.

But in finding practical solutions it is an essence to start with innocence. Innocent good people will start cleaning and working for a better earth. Awareness is the start of everything. If we do well remains a question to be seen in many years. The main answer is less. Less of gaining, less of creating, and less of wasting.

In this study I will try to proof that the equal harmony and its just representation of the trinity itself will be the real solution of the heart of the problem. But the next step will be the concrete deeds of people who know how to make things work. People who are used to work in capital organisations. People who know how to convince in a capital system. This surrender towards by study and belief is needed to finish the destruction of the earth. The end of this study will be the start of the solution. The study and the solution will be opposites for a long time. At the end it will be the ultimate solution.

Limiting quantities will be the main problem. But handling waste will be a more realistic solution in the near future and representation of the factor nature in the organisation.

2.   The self evidence of capitalism

Throughout our contest with the factor capital, the self evidence of it, will be our biggest enemy. Not for nothing mankind started to take minerals, use goods and dump them back. It was in the history of men self evident that we should use the earth. In a lesser way the animals and plants are also using the earth. The problem came with the higher intelligence of men. We were more able to use and as a result overuse the earth. Our capability is our doom.

The use of the earth was never a mayor problem. Two hundred years ago it started to become a problem. But the quadratic effect, which was known of throughout history has amazed and surprised everyone. The heart of the problem, which I describe as the quadratic effect, is the growth of the population. Never we have really believed and until this moment people still do not belief that in the year 2025, only 30 years from now, we will be with eight and a half billion. The last seventy five years the world population has grown and will grow with two hundred forty percent.

Until two hundred years the factor capital was never a real problem. This because the mere fact that the capital factor was not overwhelming. Always it has functioned with nature and men in a harmony. The self evidence as such was not only a self evidence, because of the necessity, but also because of the harmony itself. By now however the self evidence of capital is not that clear anymore. This change, also, because of the same two reasons. The first one necessity has become greed and the second one, of the original harmony is nothing left therefore the capital factor has become a problem. The necessity of capital is changed in greed for capital. Greed because people use more capital per capita. And the same greed quantity of nature has to produce more capital. Apart from the fact that people use more per capita, more people are there to use. It seems that men has a unnatural, unlimited possibility to absorb capital. It seems never ending. Also it seems, that in a polluted area, for example Mexico City, it is the most normal to invite more industry.

It is most normal and fully accepted that people representing capital units are finishing discussions with a simple "It is too expensive to pay for the consequences". It is most normal that the leading government in the world, also the biggest polluter in the world, does not want to curb pollution. Let us all hope that it will not be most normal, evidence of nature and overgrow the self evidence of men, because mankind will be swept of the earth. And this will be self evident.

2.1.   Using in harmony.

As seen before only the last two hundred years the harmony of the trinity, the harmony of the factors of existence, nature, men and capital are lost. The main reason, the quadratic effect of the overgrowth of the population. If we had seen this coming catastrophe, three hundred years ago and acted upon, maybe the world was in a better condition now. This is not the case and as a result we have to react on the present situation.

Now we have to deal with the present unbalance in harmony. As with all problems we have to make resolute changes. Changes which are going to hurt many of us, but changes which will be made in the end for the better.

The solution is as so often so very clear. and because of its clearnessit is not visible to most of us. But clear is that:
1. *There are three equal powers,*
2. *One power has overgrown the other two,*
3. *This overgrown power we have to reduce.*
Then harmony will return.

Whenever something is not used in harmony we call it an abuse. It is the abuse of the harmony which brings the not smoothed process. The world should be a smooth running process, but the false position of powers, make it go inverted. The proof of these reaction which are clearly falling out of harmony are the inverted changes. These many unnatural changes, reaction of nature, are the proof of disharmony. Many of these unnatural changes can be questioned if these will actually harm the trinity itself.

The harm, the abuse which will come, can be questioned. We can ask ourselves, what if we just go on and let happen what happens. A new harmony will rise out of the disharmony by itself. This, I think is true. But it can not be accepted, because the changes under way are of such enormous nature that mankind itself will suffer too much. As a man myself it goes against my nature. If the earth factor by itself will solve the abuse of the capital factor, it will do this by attacking the factor men.

The resulting statement, the abusing factor is capital, but only because men was the accelerator. So when harmony will come without interference of men, men will be punished and not capital. Capital will simply dissolve in its former passive state, which is equal to earth itself.

But if we men were once the accelerator we can also be the power to slow the process down. And while doing this the earth will adjust in her former place of harmony. The people who do not see the essence of world matters now, were the people who were foreseeing many problems in reference to capital limitations. In fighting these capital limitations, they were heroes for society. Now however the force of ending capital limitations is so powerful, that the opposite powers have little chance to adjust. It is of everyone's interest that these same foreseeing capitalists, are now going to become foreseeing "earth people". So the factor men which once was the hero of capitalism will now become the hero of the earth.

In stead of driving a car in a polluted overcrowded city, we will walk in between trees. This by not transporting ourselves as much and as fast. By not consuming as much and as fast. By being industrious, only in response to give back to the earth. By making active capital passive capital. Men driven by a changing hostile earth will have the power to undo what done in the last three hundred hears. We will use in harmony again and we will do everything within our powers to do it before the earth will do it by herself.

3.   The separation of capital and the organisation

Capital as the centre of capitalism. The organisation as vehicle to serve capitalism. An organisation, a form in which people act together in order to perform a shared goal. In the earth of the future, each organisation should be represented by the three factors of existence. As such it will be impossible that the organisation will only be used as a way to improve capitalism, only one factor of existence.

Because of the growth of the organisation itself, it becomes more clear that the factor capital can b separate, and become dependable, in the whole of the organisation. The production of capital in the organisation as its vehicle to achieve, are outgrown by the organisation itself. But this organisation has until now, an unchanged written goal. This goal is, to produce, to make more, to profit and to use. So it is indeed true that the society by itself has a self correction. This self correction of society has shown itself through the fact that although men has created the organisation in order to enhance capital, which is the written goal, it has become subordinate to its own vehicle. However this is not accepted by men, who created the vehicle for enlarging the capital factor and not for capital to become a dependable part of the trinity.

Rapidly we have seen that the owners of whole companies are changing in shareholders. Shareholders who represent all capital, but without a powerful vote in the organisation. This because the company has a tendency to outgrow its creators, owners. We will see this in the next paragraph. In this process it is without doubt that the relation between the provider of the capital and the actual organisation becomes in itself lesser. Apart from the distance in between capital and vehicle, also the factor men itself changed from obedience to the vehicle to a place more independent of the vehicle, although still operating from inside. So the organisation, created with capital as the goal is becoming more an institute where by now men and capital are equally represented. The third factor, the earth, is still not represented.

This self correcting process is only in a very early stage. It is true that companies have outgrown their very much divided shareholders. It is not true though that the company's organisation is represented on an equal base. It is very much the truth, that the board of directors have become more distant with the representatives of capital. At the same time it is the truth that capital has still the biggest influence in the organisation. This because the shareholders have become, in today's companies, of smaller importance as the total of creditors. These creditors all of different nature are all representatives of the factor capital. Only the factor labor has managed to force itself into the management of the organisation. By now it is honest to say that 70% is capital representation, 25% labor representation and only 5% earth representation. (these figures are an estimate without base)

The creditors of the world, the creditors of the organisation are all factors of existence on an equal base. The separation of capital and the organisation is only in the earliest stage and hard working capitalist forces are doing everything in their selfish power to turn the clock back.

3.1.   The growth of the company.

Growth is a side of the world which is a direct result of nature. It is natural, because it is the result of the growth of the world population. The growth of the company and the growth of the organisation is at the same time a result of the harmony which is already a status quo. An organisation needs to grow with the other factors of growth in order to keep what it already has within her limits. An organisation needs to grow in order to ensure her continuity. To continue her attraction to markets, capital and labor, the company needs to grow with her surrounding.

If a unit grows, its subunits become more clear. At the same time they become more limited and restricted. It is my statement, that the units of the company were until now of such a volume that the true subunits were untrue represented.

Example: A company with an investment of $ 1 million for capital goods, $ 100.000 for labor facilities, and $ 10.000 for pollution control. This company will define its budget for nature more clearly when the whole company grows 300%. In which with a relative growth in the three factors of production nature will have a budget of $ 30.000.

That this process, in which a unit could give its attention solely to capital, took thousands and thousands of years seems impossible by itself. But on the other hand until now there was never a reason to correct. The growth has reached a point, that a correction is needed. this correction shows itself in a more defined group of subunits. These growing subunits in the growing overall unit will demand each its attention.

The growth of the company is measured in quantities, as this is normal in a capitalistic purpose organisation. The quality is included in the quantity. This is the way we people have learned to measure and describe our values. It is not likely that we people will adopt an additional way to deal with values in the near future. Because of this major way in dealing with values and powers, the World Resources Institute publishes and helps with the data of the earth. This organisation has measured and counted many factors of nature never shown in such a way before, in order to present the volume of the factor nature in its true substance.

It is of enormous importance that the people see all factors of existence in a comparable way. If nature would be represented in a way more accurate to nature, it would not have the impact, it has now after changing in countable numbers.

We have to be aware that this counting of by nature uncountable factors are a very big concession to capitalism. Without any doubt we have to review this concession every so much time in order to study the possibility to change back into a more natural receiving of values.

Concession after concession will have to be made in order to adjust from a complete unbalanced organisation of life to a balance organisation of life.
The growth of the company does not only reflects the growth of the organisation. It reflects growth of population and it reflects the way people have learned how to adjust to each other. As a follow up of these adjustments it lies in the line that the adjustments of subunits will continue. The major subunits are the three powers of the organisation and as such they should come out as equals. Equals who have got the space in the organisation, because of its growth. In this we see the growth as the saviour of nature.

in the coming paragraph, capitalism is subordinate to nature, we will see that if we start again it is possible to work the other way. Less or nothing will be counted; And the smallness will ensure the factor nature. Here we will see that growth will work against nature. Never the less in the developed world, the growth of the company works in favor of the factor nature, because there is no other way. But in the developing world growth in itself will have a negative aspect, because there is still ac chance to start all over. And then it is quality we should enhance and not quantity, or growth.

3.2. Corporate raider the reason for the decline of the 80's.

Reasons for people to look to corporate raiders as evil to the society are numerous. They are driven by selfishness. They are driven by the desire or power. They are driven by their desire for more. In their attempt and realisation to get control of an organisation they ruin what has taken many years and many work. They themselves started without the capital, or very often only a few percents of the total capital. They have actually ruined to bankruptcy the biggest and best organisations. The evil these people have done in so little time has cost thousands of people hundreds of years.

Under the cover of adjusting markets, they bought with one loan, which represented capital saved in small units by many people. These companies were owned by, managed by, and laboured in by many different people. Countries saw their productivity diminish. Labourers saw their jobs going away. Savers saw their savings disappear. Banks saw their profits change in losses. Cities saw their real estate collapse. And nobody dared to point the finger, because it was only an adjustment of the market.

The quantities which are concentrated in the markets, are the centre of the counting capitalism. All materials are accompanied by their values given by the markets. The value of the shares, are already an indirect method of accounting. The fact that we people are dealing with values of values is in itself a deranged way of living. It is a fare fetched way of capitalism and the importance of these dealing diminish the importance of the other factors of production. Implausible it is that as a reaction on a market adjustment, of the value of a value, there is so much harm done to the earth. This harm is done because of the put back of progress towards a balanced organisation.

To put back capitalism is in itself a progress for nature and in a minor way for labor.

It is not my goal or other earth movements primary goal to fight capitalism, but the space needed by the earth can only be given by capitalism.

The issue of corporate raiding is the issue of a deranged and farfetched way of capitalism; To fight and accuse the accelerators of such inhuman and unearthly way of handling life is protecting harmony and the process to a better earth. The process which was under the way, the separation of capitalism and the organisation is done harm in a great way. By letting corporate raiders by complete international, huge companies, we have slid back into the history of capitalism. The provider of capital is again in a managing capacity of the organisation. In order to give back the room to nature and labor, we initially had won, it is needed to finish the way of working of the corporate raider. The decade of the eighties, the decade of the yuppies, the decade of the fall of communism has to be over. We have to return to the balancing of the organisation.

If we in fighting for the earth are concentrating all our energy on helping good movements upward, but we forget to look to deranged, farfetched ways the capitalistic factor has put upon us, we will lose in one hand, what we win in the other. Corporate raiding is such an evil.

3.3.   The suspicious shareholder.

As a normal affect on the dealings of the corporate raider, and overpaid management the little shareholder has become suspicious. They have seen enormous rises in their shares, mostly after selling them, only to see that months later the shares were worth even more. After becoming aware of the fact that their shares were unjustified undervalued for the longest time. The shares were offered back to their own availability. Now however against overvalued prices. When this had placed itself upon the small shareholder, the market tumbled in after too many harm was done to the complete stock market.

The shareholder in essence the core of capitalism, should also be helped in their organisation. Powerful organised small shareholders will help the factors nature and labor in the long run. Every organisation which is a result of al lot and small subunits, is a good organisation to work with in the future. Every organisation which has a democratic structure will help the earth movement get their equal share. This because common sense will be on the hand of equal powers. Equal powers is all we want, we do not want to wipe out capitalism, we just want our share.

The shareholder, in fact the capital holder, will help us getting it. Because they are as close to nature, as close to labor, and as close to capitalism, they are in person small representatives of the three powers.

The corporate raider or the overpaid manager has little or no relation with nature or labor, simply because his share in the capitalistic factor in unreasonable and undemocratic big. His personality is unbalanced and so will be his decisions.

The fact that many people have shares and many people have direct access to corporate decisions is positive. The world can be saved if capital is equally divided, but the truth of capitalism is the unequal division. Every man on earth should have some capital, should do some labor, and should be involved in some nature. Men will bring his wisdom to the organisation.

All former limits and frontiers should be broken, in order to form new and just organisations. It is very well possible that the European Community and its equals are just a step in between an even more harmonious organisation. However to break the old unjust frontiers of the national governments it is needed to go towards a European Community. Every habitant should share in the responsibility of leading on an equal base the community towards government on nature, capital and labor.

Suspicion will be an include part of bearing responsibility. Now it is the task of the suspicious shareholder to accuse the corporate raider and overpaid manager. Their guilt is conspiring against the shareholders loss, but also against the put back of progress in the movement of the earth.

3.4. Debts and credits not based on capital.

In our today world debts and credits are expressed in currencies and known values. Movable materials are easy to be counted and easy to be measured. Capital is easy to represent on the balance sheet, in these currencies and values.

Labor and nature are more difficult to count and more difficult to measure. For capital in that time it seemed impossible to place these intangible, at that time not even assets, on the balance sheet.

When labor became a more dominant force into the organisation, we learned to measure the intangible assets. The intangible assets and liabilities became an issue when labor became an issue in the organisation. The value of good labor, the value of research and the value of certain managers were materialised. From that moment the capitalistic world understood labor. They saw it in figures. Figures they could sell. Figures they could place on their balance sheet.

Now we are about fifty years later. now we struggle with the same problem, we have to materialise nature. This in order to represent it on the balance sheet. We do not want to name it intangible, but to go easily over in tangibles, maybe it is needed to convince the people who represent the capital factor. We the earth people are counting and measuring, completely against everything we belief, only to convince the capitalists in their own language.

In the United States is developed a program which is typically for this very capitalistic country. They have found a way to measure and count different forms of pollution. A certain quantity of different kinds of pollution is named under a collective noun. This collective noun is made a unit. For these units the North Americans have formed a market. Every producing organisation is given, by a committee, a certain amount of units, according to a certain way of distribution. When productive organisation is classified as a heavy polluter, but is a clean and not polluting organisation, because of internal programs, then this supposed polluter has units in excess. The company can sell these units. Other companies will need more units, because they are more polluting as they were allowed to. These units in excess and these units in demand will come together in this specially created market. So the result is that companies have legal ways to pollute more then allowed, but they will have to pay the market price for it.

This solution is a good solution for the time being. It makes that the polluter pays and the non polluter gets the credit. The only way the capitalistic world will understand their guilt in doing harm to the earth is when they can read it on their balance sheet in hard currency. the polluter pays. And it is not so that we do not know who the polluter is. Everyone who brings up the question "Who is the polluter?" makes himself guilty of holding up the process. The polluter is the one who pollutes. Not the one who enjoys the polluter's product. Only with an assumption like this the road to clearness is within our limits. Indirect of course the consumers will pay, but direct the polluter pays. The limitation of the complexity will bring the solution. It is of utmost importance that we will limit and bring clearness in the complex world of earthly movements. If this can be done by making it readable to capitalistic organisations and people, then this is a low price to pay.

The values which have to represent the earth are as in the capitalistic world to be divided in liabilities and assets or as debts and credits. The right to pollute will be a credit. The obligation to clean will be a debt. The need to dump will be a debt. The possibility to recycle will be a credit. The companies by themselves need to give values to these debts and credits. The best thing would be if they would do this without obligations from outside. This however will be a farfetched dream. We need to accelerate the process of bringing the earth into the picture again. We need to bring the earth into the balance sheet. How contradictory this may seem.

4.   Capital as a way to equalise

When communism became a power to give recognition to, in the beginning of the twentieth century, it was generally seen as an equalising power. However it did not work, it could not work. It was not an equalising power, because people are not equal. People are different and they will always be different. Communism made the same mistake as capitalism. They thought they could organise without the other factors of existence. In their fight against capitalism, they deliberately left all capital issues out of their organisation; this by itself was a grave mistake, since it is not possible to leave any factor of production out.

The biggest mistake they made however, was the fact that they were so primary in their efforts to start a society, that they did not include, at all the factor nature. Now we see that this had much bigger influences in their failure as the fact that they have left out capitalism. The left overs of this utterly pathetic grasp for power, we will pay for much longer then the whole existence of their pitiful empire. It is a grave shame on this earth that a movement which could be a perfect example, for the old capitalistic world. That they have failed basically only, because of their desire for greatness and power. That what should have been a sample of a different possible way of life has simply out of desire for competition. Competition so much an capitalistic ideal. Let us learn out of the mistakes labor made and let the earth movement be more smart.

But the point I try to make is, however it is communism which had the name of equalising, capitalism has brought it to us. Communism has failed to work with capitalism and has failed to work with nature. Their only interest was mankind. This is elementary wrong, because the world exists out of three different factors of existence. Capitalism at least has managed to include the factor labor in its organisation for the last seventy years. And is much more involved in bringing in the factor nature. I see communism as much greater creator of classes and as such, as a much bigger evil. In a way communism has brought the opposite as it had promised. But a different opposite, still an opposite to capitalism, but not the one they had spoken about. Again it was a wrong way, again it was a unbalanced society.

Capitalism is more equalising, because its companies have grown so enormous, that equality became a result. In the fight between communism and capitalism the emphasis was always on the action of the difference in governments. In the meantime however companies were fulfilling major tasks in the capitalistic societies. It were these capitalistic companies, who brought the equality the communist government was so eagerly looking for.

They brought equality in products. They brought equality in work force. They brought equality in production facilities. They brought equality in entire consumer patrons. I find it positively remarkable that the providers of classes have so encouraged equality. While in the meantime the providers of equality have put back their own classless society by starting and encouraging an unbalanced organisation.

The reason I think positively about equalising is not because I accept equality in human beings themselves. But because I think a more homogeneous society has more possibilities to survive in a more hostile earth.

This should not be the case when population was within the limits of two hundred years ago. Now however we are with an enormous quantity of people, that homogeneous population can offer the only solution towards an more smooth organisation. And as so a more balanced society.

4.1. By needs.

Human beings have natural equality in needs. They need food, housing, and luxurious capital goods. Without any help from constitution or obligation from government, people tend to equality much more as to inequality. Of course it is true that people are all different in nature, but the consonances are absolutely dominant.

Because of their needs, they ask the industry the same products, they ask the same way of distribution and they ask, in a way, the same kind of advertising. All these similar needs lead to an even more homogeneous group of people. Therefore we can not blame communism for making the world a dull and boring group of homogeneous people. The capitalistic world itself has much more contributions to an equal world as the communistic world, who enhance equality through constitution.

4.2. By process.

Again it is the same, because of a certain process, people are forced into equality. By needs they voluntarily join the commonplace. By process it is more out of need, for payable luxury goods, that people tend to become more equal. It is out of need for bringing commonplace goods to all people, that the process of production is doomed to bring equality.

The process of winning, producing, distributing and advertising goods is making capitalism an accelerator in promoting a more equal society. Since growth is such a major force in the development processes in goods. They are accumulated and put on the same level, in order to bring these goods to as much, as possible, people. The process of bringing numbers together will make goods available to the people. The capitalistic process equals more as the communistic process.

4.3. By market.

Not by constitution, but by market more then anything else, people show their desire for equality. All over the world people drink coca cola, et MacDonald's, use French perfume and Swedish furniture, they drive Japanese cars and listen to Korean radios. The market is a common market. It is a direct wish of all kind of industries and capitalistic governments to create common markets. The profit of the industry lies in the commonplace of people. Normalcy will turn out to be the saviour of the earth.

In addition to the self evidence of human equality, a main product of capitalism has enhanced equality more then anything else. This product is transportation. Transportation of humans and transportation of information, which we call communication. These two products of fast progress have lead to an enormous process of promoting an equal society. Since communism was not able to perform, capitalism has brought equality to the world by its creation of and its market for transportation and communication.

5.   Capital subordinate to the trinity

Capital is everything which can be moved around the word. Capital is material created by men, created to serve men. The trinity stands for the factors capital, labor and nature together. These three factors of existence form together the unit to perform, the unit of existence, the unit of production. This unit I call the trinity.

Until now the trinity itself was subordinate to capital. This was a consequence of thousands and thousands of years of human creations. This became the capital mistake. In the beginning it was a harmless harmony, but when growth became predominating a new harmony should have been appeared. This adjusted harmony until today's world is not yet been established. According to me in this study, everything which went wrong on this earth is a direct result of the unbalanced trinity; from the first economic studies done on earth, people who follow the capitalistic example, have acknowledged nature, labor and capital as equal powers of importance. Somewhere along the line however the capitalistic factor has gained more importance as its counterparts, nature and labor.

It is not my wish to dominate capitalism, but as a third part of the trinity it should, in the future, rest in the created harmony. The goals and ways of working can differ from organisation to organisation; However the democratic decision forming should be based on people representing in an equal vote, nature, labor and capital; As such it is without a doubt that capital should obey to labor and nature. This is no essential problem, since labor has as much in common with capital, as nature has in common with capital as labor has in common with nature. The trinity is an equal one and there are no superiors. That is, there should be no superiors.

5.1.   Capital subordinate to labor

What labor has tried to do in the beginning of the twentieths century, in the Eastern European countries was the creation of a society. A society where capital was subordinate, it was completely ignored in the whole society. Capital was seen as a force which should serve mankind. Nature was seen as a force which should serve mankind. All powers were subordinate to mankind. It is because of this unbalanced society that it failed.

No power will allow itself to be subordinate to an other power. No power will serve an other power. Powers should serve each other. Powers should be equal. People have measured powers in a for people convenient way. If this way of measuring the powers was accurate, towards the powers themselves was never questioned. Now the time and power reaction have learned us that we have made mistakes in measuring the powers. If the following is true or untrue we do not know,

Is nature a lesser power than labor.
Is nature a lesser power then capital.
Is labor a lesser power then nature.
Is labor a lesser power then capital.
Is capital a lesser power then nature.
Is capital a lesser power then labor.

The only possible way to handle these unknown factors of existence are to give them each equal recognition. The possibility to count or the impossibility to count of powers is more powerful then the other power. Capital is as forceful as labor and as such will not be subordinate to labor.

5.2.   Capital subordinate to nature.

The basics of the former paragraph can also be implied on this paragraph. But in the former paragraph we have seen how capital subordinate to labor was of importance with the communist revolution. Now we will see that capital subordinate to nature is of great importance to the developments in the developing world.

To help developing in the developing world is a much more difficult task as we ever could have imagined. When we started to exploit, we called it development. Now we are still exploiting, and we still call it development. Probably to exploit is the same as to develop, this is a true possibility.

The development of the developing countries could be the development of the developed countries and the exploitation of the developed countries could be the exploitation of the developing countries.

The law of the strongest is hard to deny. Still the developed world is developing the developing world and the fact that we continue is a positive fact. After all it is not all that easy. And their always remains the question who is to blame? The todays developers, or the old developers? The todays locals or the old locals? This however, is a different study.

Recent studies have let us known that helping developing countries is most successful on a very small scale. It has proven successful only when adopted to the local people themselves. The bigger the organisations, the bigger the failures. It are the people themselves who should be helped at the very bottom of society. The people have to learn how to start a society together with nature and capital. For me the problem of failures the bigger organisation have known and still know, find their origin in the fact that they are unbalanced.

The very same problems as in the capitalistic world, where capital plays a role too dominant. The very same problems as in the communistic world, where men play a role too dominant. In the developing world the problem rises, because the earth movement tries to let nature have too dominant a role. All these are wrong, because organisations should have equal representations for nature, labor and capital. The reason why small scale, down to earth, developments work is because in these smaller societies or organisations it come natural that the three factors of existence are represented equal. This we can also see in our own early historical societies. The smaller the organisation the more natural it is to have a balanced organisation. The bigger the organisation the easier it is for essential wrong growing of factors of existence.

2. Organising labor.

The self evidence of capital is that what the tree factors of production started with thousands of years ago. Only one century ago the representation of labor became a fact. Now, at a moment when these two powers, capital and labor, have found a certain way of working along sides, the third power, nature comes in; Because labor is such a young addition the harmony, we the earth movement can learn a lot out of the organisation of labor. This organisation started only in the beginning of this century, and as such a lot of information and studies are to our availability. The labor movement went in many ways the same path as the path nature has to follow.

In the today's organisations the earth movement has a lot to thank to the labor movement; Because until now the factor nature was never represented, the factor labor has often taken this responsibility within its own movement. Labor unions often saw it in their advantage to use nature in their fight against capital. The labor unions saw the protection of nature as a protection of men n the productive companies. However on the long run nature will need its own representation.

On the long run labor will become as much an opposite to nature as capital will be. Or as much a cooperating power as capital will be.

Today however we are glad that in certain fights labor is on natures side. Today it is hard to see and understand that nature will take from labor as vigorously as capitals has always taken from labor.

The labor movements within the democratic societies have given the word the clear proof that it is possible to work with more then one power along sides. The pie is still unfair divided and labor still has the right to a bigger piece. But certain pars, which now fall within the labor movement belong to the nature movement. These newly won powers will have to be handed over to the new power earth. This in itself will be not easy, but necessary. Each power will have to represent itself and not the rights of the cooperating power. It is from utmost importance that each factor of existence will defend her own interests. If this will not happen a clear representation will never be.

The following question will be difficult to answer. The following question is: How do we involve democratic decision making in on forehand equal trinity? This is not an easy question. But a diminishing earth is an even greater danger, then a difficult question.

So the democratic solution will be that every vote will have to be made in triple. One vote for nature. One vote for capital. And one vote for labor. Every woman and every man will have to bring three votes.

The liberty of democracy will have to learn to go hand in hand with the trinity. The authority of capitalism will have to be replaced with the authority of the trinity.

2.1. Coming together

In the beginning of the century labor started to move by inviting people of a similar interest. These people would come together in little bars and café's to discuss their faith. To discuss the way it had to happen. To discuss their fight against capitalism.

Now the earth movement is doing the same; They come together a little more adopted to this time, but still they come together. Everything goes different, now we use television, books, computers and stickers. But at the same time our opponents are using the same means of communication. Which has forced us to use capitalistic ways to get earthly goals.

1.   By groups of mutual interests.

All people who were labouring felt suppressed. They lived in poor housing, they had no adequate food, they had no medical attention and they had no time off. The difference between the upper class and the lower class was enormous and basically there were no classes in between. The then existing organisations were capital, religious or governmental organisations and each of them were representing the capital factor of existence. The self evidence of capitalism started because some people were more smart as others. But the world changed and the world was growing. This leaded to a small superior upper class, which inherited the growing capital power. The working class, lower class, became bigger and bigger and poorer and poorer. It took thousands of years to reach this unbalanced society, but when the point was reached it worked quadratic. The working class, mainly because of numbers became powerful. The capital class had to start give recognition to something what they never even had noticed.

It was as many things in life a circle. Because of the growth of the population, which was mainly lower class, capital had to produce more. More people and younger people had to work and produce more. At the same time capitalists became fewer and the working class grew and became poorer. Because of the work which was exaggerating, the labor class could not follow anymore. It was not so much that they did not want to, but they were not capable anymore with keeping up with the exaggerating capital factor. The more people, the more production, the more capital, the circle is complete.

Children had to work too early, women had to work too much and the men had to work for too little reward. They started to talk together and felt the same about the injustice. They saw the owners, the representatives of capitalism as the evil. This was true, because these representatives of capitalism were no people anymore, they themselves had become the power of capitalism. They had changed from men into capital. From a human being they changed into material. They were materialised. The capitalist did not see it that way, and they needed to be corrected by their servants. By the servants of mankind. These servants came together and bound their mutual power against capital.

2.   By democratic vote.

Labor came into power by democratic vote. Capital kept a lot of the power because of the on their hand religious parties. By now governmental organisations are very much representing labor and capital on a equal base. Strangely enough the two of them together have developed a way of mutual understanding which leads to suppressed earth. The factor nature is the victim of the cooperation of labor with capital. (Even when we have seen in the former paragraph 2, that labor has been helping the earth movement). When labor first came into political power, they called themselves communists. The communist party was a party which wanted capital completely out. Recent history has learned us the disastrous affect of labor trying to manage the whole organisation. Now the communist parties have become socialist parties and are cooperating within the capitalist system.

Of course the labor movement would not like to hear that they are playing a minor role in today's society. Labor has very often more or equal votes then capital, but is does not translate into actual power for labor. The overpowering force is clear and still the factor of capital. In my view it needs more then one new power to overthrow an old power. In my view when the power earth comes in they will team up with labor to overthrow the overpowering force of capital. Also, because of the setback of the labor movement in Eastern Europe, labor has not the power stated, they should have been stating by now. This all to become equal and separate powers in the end.

Only when labor had actual representation in government and in the productive organisations themselves, which they got thanks to democracy. The democracy in the Western world was basically the counterpart of communism in the Eastern countries. After democracy had stated sin labor could start breaking old rules. Ownerships had to be divided, labor rewards had to rise, and social securities had to be founded. Freedoms had to be established and time had to be transported from capitalism to men.

All these decisions were made as if the third power, nature did not exist and it is therefore that a lot of these decisions have to be reexamined in the present society.

The society as it is existing at this moment has to be reexamined, as if the three and not the two powers of existence, are representation the today's organisations. Awareness of real importances. Awareness of the democratic power is what has to bring humans toward the authority to the trinity.

3.   By force.

On the moment the democratic force is installed, power can be directed from above. And such a power can not be overlooked. The labor parties have installed many laws after they took power in the government. This does not mean that there were no laws favouring labor at all before these labor parties came in power. Capitalist parties have written and brought into power, laws which were favouring labor. Whey these capitalist parties had done so, is not exactly known. But for example keeping labor within limits of keeping labor happy for the time being, could be good reasons. Also in today's government we see the same things happening towards the not yet represented earth movements. Even a not represented nature gets laws in favour of its movement.

For example in The Netherlands there is a law, which tells projects of a certain nature, to develop a report (M.E.R.) before starting the project. This report measures the affects for nature, before the project is developed. This law as many other laws of an earthly nature are installed and written by existing parties. These parties are not necessarily parties, who represent the earth. In a situation where there is a lack of a certain power another power will fill the gap. This is of course honourable, but it is not a permanent solution. Every power has a right to be represented by their own being, a true balanced society can develop.

Force is needed to install a power, which until now was not a part. But forcing a point of view, a point of power on a society is dangerous. It is dangerous for the power which is enforcing itself. The same example of the Environmental affect report (M.E.R.) can show us why it is endangering for the earth self. Organisations which are planning a project have to develop this report. But since the guidelines of this report are so unclear to all involved parties, nobody knows exactly what the content of this report has to be. The guidelines are unclear, because the parties involved are forced to be involved. So the report itself, when made can form not a protection for the earth, but a protection for the capital factor. Naturally it is true that the instalment of the report is only positive, but we have to study if the aspect of forceful imposing does not work against the enforcing power. To force upon can always work in the opposite of the initial promotion.

2.   Problems to face

To bring a power on a field, which is occupied with an other power, gives problems. It will open a justified fight. And this fight is justified, because the occupying power has the right of custom. This right of custom is the right won by the time the other powers have allowed, the occupying power to rule. On the other hand the fight will be justified, because the new power was too long absent. This absent power was missed and the very fact that it seeks the field for appearance is the proof of missing. Both powers have the right to defend the field. Each power will have their support and each power will have their rightful share in the end.

The old power is capital, the power we talk about in this chapter is labor. The power which is coming in at this very moment is earth. It is my belief that the today's division of these three powers are unbalanced in order to continue the world we know. The world we know, the world we want. The part labor has claimed, was and is belonging to the labor. The part which will be claimed by earth belongs to the earth. Therefore no real opposition can form a real threat.

2.1.   Awareness of the problem.

When labor started to move into capital, no capital representatives were aware of any malfunctioning of their organisation. Now we are seventy five years later, and still the labor movement needs to win some field. And still many capital representatives are not aware of problems, which are caused by a not representative share of labor in the total organisation.

In today's world the biggest problem again is the awareness of the problem. Labor as well as nature lack pure existence.

The location of the problem and the extent of the problem. This plays on both sides. On one side labor and nature are not completely aware of any problems and on the other side capital is not aware of any problems.

The capital factor was and is more responsible for the present earthly problems. This because they were able in spirit and material, and being so, they had the possibility to be aware. If they indeed were aware is not sure. That they had the capability to know and be aware of the extent and location of the problem is sure. The labor movement was mostly unaware out of incapability in spirit and material. Therefore they were not as responsible for letting the world be unnecessarily long in an unbalanced society. But as a result of this knowledge within the capital factor. It were indeed the insiders of capitalism, but not necessarily people who agreed with capitalism, who started to acknowledge the problem of lacking the factor labor. Very often these critical capitalists were the initiators of the labor movement.

For labor self it was even harder to acknowledge the problem. They were involved in their commonplace life and were not aware of other opportunities. Apart from their own unawareness they walked against a strong defence of capital. They were the first to defy capital and never this had happened before. Capital till now, had always made out life.

Never anywhere in the world the factor capital had encountered any major defeats, because there was simply never an opposite power.

Some countries in the world had of course a more labor friendly society, but almost all countries had a capital directed society. Apart from the Eastern communist countries, which by now as we have seen have failed. This failure was only a result of not acknowledging capital and nature as power as well. As a result of this failure these communist countries are now again tending to the old capitalist system. This is a step backwards.

To become aware of a problem one has to miss something. One has to be unhappy about something. The people who had done the work, the people who had laboured for capital were becoming unhappy. This unhappiness has lead to the location of possible problems.
The major problem they, the labourers, came upon were the class differences. This inequality made them unhappy. People who were basically the same, noticed an enormous gap between men, the ones who were working, and the ones who were representing capital. Like everything else, also this grew out of normalcy and out of tolerance, because of the universal growth in the world. The labor in the capital language, the stage of awareness for all problems and now the most pressing problem is the suppressed earth. We have to become aware.

2.2.   Existing class system.

What exists, is concurred, and what is concurred is a power. The existing class system was and is a power, which has taken place in a certain field. This field will not be surrendered without a fight. The field we are talking about is the society or the organisation. This class system is the core of unhappiness for many, even not labourers. The uneven division of capital and rights of freedom is the reason for unhappiness and problems. That what exists has to go, because the world has grown out of the existing stability. However it is human to accept differences. Humanity has separated themselves from other creatures of nature, because of differences. It was the use of materials, which indicated intellect, and started differences. Therefore now we have differences in people, and as a result a class system.

As every other existence of a quantity, also the class system will have to make room for a more qualitative solution. In this overcrowded world there is simply no room anymore for a system based on classes. It is not an attack on this system itself, but it just a too much space occupying system. The smaller upper class is simply not capable anymore to keep the always bigger becoming, lower class within their limits.

The growth of he world can only be managed, when the quality of the organisation becomes more detailed. Only when quality keeps track with quantity, the world can be saved.

At this moment quality does not keep track with quantity. That in itself is only normal, because adjustments are continuously needed. Now, however it is only normal that we adjust the quality to the level of quantity. In order to do so we have to count and measure these different powers, because that will be the only possibility to put them on equal levels.

The way labor has worked to eliminate the class system, was not always satisfying, but they have done not badly also. Now the labor movement has still some way to go and the earth movement starts to get power. With these combined powers it will be easier to get the rightful piece of the pie. The way to accomplish will be enhancing structural changes. I reproach the present representatives of nature, of not bringing in their power in a more structural sense. In my view real results can only be booked, when the changes are structural and not on the surface. The labor movement did a lot of structural organising to get their share. We, the earth movement, have to learn from them. There is no doubt that it is of essential importance that awareness is the first problem to face. This awareness we accomplish by numerous actions directed to big groups of people, who are not immediate responsible for structural changes. But once the awareness is a fact and present, it is of utmost importance that the changes will be of organisational tendency. For these changes the time has come as well for labor as for nature. The essence is the heart of the society and this are the organisations. In these organisations power has to be divided equal in between men, capital and earth. The capital class system is a organisational limitation to get the desired balanced society.

In addition to this paragraph, which shows the negative sides of the class system more then the positive sides. It is needed for me to commend on the possibilities for a positive class system within a balanced world. It is my opinion that the organisations and societies have to ensure equal representation of men, earth and capital. In doing so all organisations and societies will become similar and maybe sometimes boring. This, because it is organised and not the law of the strongest.

The law of the strongest is an out of date principle, which can not function in the today's world.

However this law of the strongest is generally seen as a more exiting way of life for which many people have chosen. But what is well possible within a balanced society is different people. It is not because the society is highly organised that the people can not differ from each other.

For example: We can compare this with the European Community. Because the European Community is a highly organised society, which brings together many sub-societies, these former sub-societies can differ even more from each other.

Even so these sub-societies can become greater in quantity. Here we see again if quality grows, quantity can grow. Class systems in a whole will disappear, but difference in people will be allowed in the new society. So the excitement of life will be ensured by the growing differences in between people.

2.3.   No existing infrastructure.

The problems to face, are apart from the opposing powers themselves, also the not existing infrastructure. The infrastructure which is existing, is the infrastructure which is supporting the existing system. The existing system is the system which serves the capital factor. In order to win field it is needed to have an infrastructure, which allows the entrance. The infrastructure we can call the road to get there. The road allows us the entrance. The existing organisations were only organised in such a way that only the capital factor could use them.

Labor could not use this infrastructure, because this road, these organisations did not allow labor, the entrance. Only when labor had installed the unions, the support groups and the political labor parties. Only then the infrastructure was available to this secondary system, the system which allows labor, start coming in. The way the labor movement went to work was by starting talk in groups and political meetings and so, making the people aware of their rights. It found support and more people joined the labor forces. If at such meetings the labor movement had not found support the movement would have been an impossible future power. It was because of its support that labor proofed to be a major future power.

Even in capital strongholds like the United States of America the labor movement became a power which was respected. The United States of course never went very far in giving space to the labor factor. The fact that the United States are a stronghold for capitalism is easy to understand, if we study the geographical richness and space of the United States. These give the North Americans the power of space for a still enlarging capitalistic system. Also we can study the recent history of the United Stated, which allows the North Americans to be younger then the old European continent. The still available space and the fresh start in the New world gives a stronger capitalism as in the Old world.

Never the less the American labor unions are one of the most powerful in the world and one of the most respected by the capitalistic companies and judicial system. This is mainly to thank to the goof infrastructure the democratic system allows.

This existing infrastructure, installed for the purposes of capitalism, could be used and is used also by the new labor movement.

in Europe, we have see, that labor has taken over complete governments. This was in most cases the only possibility, since the existing infrastructure did not allow any other power as the capital power to use it. The infrastructure very often was so bad, that it was simply impossible for the labor no road to find. For example the organised crime in Italy has troubled the infrastructure in this country. For this the combined economic powers can be a solution. In Europe the European Community can allow an entrance to the earth movement. But as well to the still needed bigger power, for the labor movement the European Community can be a solution. The combined economic powers will bring the needed infrastructure to all the countries involved. The combined powers will bring the needed infrastructure to all the countries involved. The infrastructure will be the road to welfare of men, earth and capital.

2.4.   Internal differences.

Apart from the problems, which arise because of competing powers there are also the problems formed within their own about the way to go and the goal to reach within their own groups and members. Some people are ore moderate, some people are more radical. One group is in favor of fast changes and the other group is in favour of slow changes. These are the differences, in the way how to accomplish certain goals. Next to the differences in the way, there are the differences in the goal. For labor the overall goal will be that man has to be represented. But the minor goal, therefore can differ enormously. In one country for example total communism will be chosen. In an other country a political party, next to capitalist parties and religious parties, can be chosen as goal to accomplish. These differences in how to work and the goal to reach can bring internal differences.

More specific we can see that in the factor labor the following divisions were made in the past and in the present. The religious labor movements, the intellectual labor movements, the communistic labor movements, the feminist labor movements, the socialistic labor movements. All these groups had only one goal in common and that was and is the factor human had to be respected in the society and the organisation. All these groups had different opinions on how to go to work and how to accomplish this common goal. But as you see every labor movement has included in their name and spirit a second nature; This second nature could be in fact the first nature. For example a Catholic labor party could well give major concessions towards capitalism in their fight against it, if this particular deal would give more recognition to Catholicism then an opposing deal, which would give more recognition to labor. From party to party, but also from decision to decision, it was and is, always a question which nature of the group will be served. The internal differences were often include in the nature and name of the group.

As a whole the very fact of the many different groups to work towards the same goal will encourage differences. These differences can only be solved in an overhanging organisation, which will bring the common goals together. This summarising of complexity will have to happen, without the input of the secondary natures or goals. This higher organisation. Other humanitarian natures will be secondary or without any influence. The problems to face from outside or inside will be solved by denying them. Of course here I presume that these secondary powers will let themselves being denied. If this would not be the case, then this should not happen.

My whole study can only win field if no other powers as labor, nature and capital will fight for the world.

And it is my honest opinion that no other powers will claim the world. Everybody will understand and see there is no room anymore for an other division.

3.   Equal representation

By now labor is a part of many companies, many governments and many foundations. Nobody makes decisions without thinking about the people who actually do the work. Nobody makes decisions about the people who do the work without involving them in the problem. If airlines are going to be taken over by a competitor, one of the first questions will be, what will the reaction be of the unions. The unions for pilots, ground personal and stewards have a major vote in the takeover of a capitalistic enterprise. If the Dutch government is going to move their headquarters for the postal system, the first people to talk with are the employees. Without their influence and support the move will be an impossibility. If an out of date factory in Europe will be closed by the corporation, this can only happen f for all employees are found replacing jobs or sufficient compensation. These examples show the successful representation of labor in the capitalist system.

On the other hand although, there is no equal representation. The representation is a fact, but we are still a far way from an equal vote in decision making, especially at the business corporation. On the average board of directors there is still no member which is unique responsible for labor matters. Few corporations feel the necessity to publish a social annual report. Few corporations feel the necessity to involve voluntarily the labourers in major company decisions. In no company goal there will be mentioned the progress of labor together with the profit and continuation of the capital factor.

The only goal of every corporation in the Western world is still the profit and continuation of capital.

If labor as really accepted as an equal partner, there would be as many members of labor as members of capital on the board directors. Together with other proofs of acceptance by the capital factor.

Groups of people, governments, parties, corporations, foundations and religious institutions need to be represented on an equal base as well by capitalism as by labor. By now we know a third factor, a third power will have to play a role. The role of the earth, which will take its part in the decision of the future. Every unit of togetherness will have labor, nature and capital in their goals.

Every company will have the purpose to:
1. ensure the continuation of humans,
2. ensure the continuation of capital,
3. ensure the continuation of the earth.

As we see apart from the three goals instead of one, we also leave out the growing factor. (more about this in the next paragraph) These three goals will ensure equal representation.

3.1. The dominance of capital.

The fact that capital has a dominant role in our present society is explained in the paragraph, the self evidence of capitalism. Here we will discuss why the factor capital is dominant to the factor labor. The organisational essence of this problem finds itself mainly in the position of the purposes of the companies. The companies, corporations or enterprises are the main group of the today's organisation.

All these capitalistic organisations are based on getting more capital. In the eighties the world became even so capitalistic, that the essence continuation became of minor importance. Only the growth factor was essential for a company, which would be called a project. The temporary project was winning field of the continuous corporation. Capital became in this evolution even more important and dominant over the other two factors of production.

The dominance of capital is represented by written goals divided in two major parts.

1. The growth of the capital.
2. The continuation of the vehicle in which the capital knows it's growth.

Growth as we know by now is the major wrong for the factor earth. Apart from the denial of the earth, these purposes also do not mention the factor labor. For a vehicle, organisation or corporation, which exist thanks to the science of economics, this is very strange. Strange because it is this science, which starts with explaining the three powers of economics; Labor, Earth and Capital. It is this science, which and of equal strength. But to come back on the goal we see that continuation is of importance to the vehicle. Within the continuation we as optimistic could find a hint towards earth and labor. This since we know that continuation of the corporation is only possible if the power labor and nature are rewarded. Now however we see in the last decennial a tendency to leave the second part of the goals, the continuation also behind.

In the eighties we have seen that big multinational and national corporations have first separated and later sold many of the original tasks of the corporation. This method of working brings the corporation in an always narrower field of work. As a result this original major corporation has positioned itself in such a way that only the growth of capital is the essence. If this corporation would have had social responsibilities towards a certain local society, then it has narrowed itself out of these responsibilities.

To narrow a company down, is in a world were responsibilities have to be seen, a major crime.

In the eighties we have seen that apart from the narrowing down of corporations, the continuation of these corporation have become of minor importance, in contradiction to the growth of the capital. We sere capital being moved from one unit to an other unit. We see the biggest companies going bankrupt as if it did not have taken them three hundred years to become. We see major accomplishments in the capital factor being done by a corporation specially erected for this one time project. We see complete factories open and close within a five year period, for which the goals were as such written down in a temporary agreement. We see the dominance of capital becoming more and more important. It is frightening how the factor capital can be so involved with itself. It is frightening how the capital factor can be so ignoring to their own growth, which is crushing humans and earth together.

2. The lack of nature.

It is because labor is a new power fighting for space with capital the old power. It is because capital has already so much more field then labor, that it is difficult for labor to win additional field. The lack of a third power, which could help the new power labor, is obvious. The lack of something. The lack of the power. the fact that there is something missing in the present harmony. And it is, as it is so often, very obvious. We are lacking too much nature. We are missing the silence of nature. We are missing the space of nature. We are missing the greenery of nature. We are missing the diversity of nature. We are missing the cleanness of nature. We are missing the openness of nature. We are missing the water, air and earth of nature. People feel without the knowing factor the lack of the power nature. It is this missing feeling which will make the power grow.

More concrete, we can say that this missing feeling will eventually lead towards a representation of earth. The labor movement will miss an accompanying force to fight capitalism. Capitalism is able to fight labor, because capital fights for freedom and differences in people. Freedom and differences are more wanted goals as the goals labor fights for. Labor fights for equality and a more dull society. But now comes nature. Nature represents no dullness. Nature represents no filth. Nature represents no equality. Nature represents no strings. Nature will give labor the force needed to come in and justify its selfishness. Selfishness because labor fights for people, so people fighting for people. Nature will give capital the possibility to justify their retreat without losing face. Because the capitalists will bring with the help of their money the loveliness of nature back to the people. Nature will gibe the solution to both, because its lack in the present.

3. The impossibility of the equilibrium.

The verb to balance means by itself that there will be no complete standstill. The fact that there will always be some movement is therefore an act of normalcy. We call the factor of labor, the power of labor, in which power means energy and energy means movement. Therefore the labor movement, the earth movement and the capital movement. The last one is not so much known as a movement, since they are the established power, which does not want to move.

In the past the equilibrium was a fact. Capital was not too big a power next to earth and men. The world had enough space to allow people to be industrious and to allow people to grow in quantity. There was enough nature to absorb the coming power capital.

In the past there was enough nature also to absorb the growing population.

If we look into history we see that it is only recently that the earth could not cope anymore with the overpopulation. The balance is lost and the impossibility of the equilibrium is not a result of the natural position of the society, but a result of the overpopulation.

If we assume that we can live in an equilibrium with the present population and this indeed we assume. Even more so we assume that we can grow for another thirty five years, until we have reached eight and a half billion people. And even with these astronomical population we think we can manage the earth. Because the summit in Rio of June 1992, was focused on this growth, where the sustainable growth was the essence. The sustainable growth is the stable point where we want to keep the world. It is a growth which allows continuation. It is not a growth in quantity, but a growth in quality. Possible or not the world will have to find the balance. This balance we will get by giving back to nature what we have taken. By giving to the people what we take from them. By taking from capital what we have given capital. Or by finding an equilibrium and keeping the three powers stable.

2.   The controlling task of labor

We have seen that labor has taken certain tasks of the earth movement for their own account. This was done because the earth had no representation in the past, and capital did not seem to notice the earth's needs. If labor did this out of real care for the earth or just felt that this representation could help their own movement we do not really know. But it is safe to assume that within the labor movement there were people who noticed the earth's needs. On the other hand it was of course also true that the movement felt that two powers had more influence then one power.

Selfishness is natural commonplace for (independent) powers.

Even labor, who cares for people, will only take care of people and not for the earth. But when a certain power is not represented there is a vacuum and this vacuum will be filled with an other energy. In this case labor took the vacuum, which as we can see now, of nature.

However today, the earth movement has more to thank then to reproach to the labor movement. Many organisations with a labor origin are now working for the earth movements. Many organisations critical on the capital corporations, started as a part of the unions of labor. These unions were critical on every move of the companies, and as such in the best position to criticise. Criticising on the capital facto, not only because space taken from nature. The political labor parties together with the labor unions were at one time the only defenders of the earth. They defended men general. This included men in the developed world. They defended men, which included the environment of men.

The controlling tasks done by the labor movement manifests itself in numerous subdivisions of he movement. We can give the following research material, which is among others available at the political and corporate labor movement.

As examples: 1. Solidarity in between developed and developing countries,
2. Contribution of mass media towards becoming conscious in solidarity and the general labor movement.
3. The evolution and control of multinational corporations,
4. The evolution of the feminist movement, in developing world,
5. Availability of comparisons of goods to the consumers,
6. The importance of environment in general.

These are just some examples of what the labor movement is involved in. At this moment the environment is only a study, which is important, because it borders the interests of labor.

2.4.1   Together with government.

On the same level as the government, certain non governmental organisations can have the same functions as the government. These non governmental organisations, very often foundations, either brought into life by the government itself or by the private section, operate in order to control the big multinational corporations. They do this by gathering information, good as well as bad, about the all important multinationals. The information they distribute, in order to bring awareness to the people.

Since the multinational is working over the borders of independent countries, no real controlling power can be authorised over these enterprises.

It is of enormous importance, because the multinational often is the only one who has direct supervision over its field of work. No country is solely responsible, not even an economic community is solely responsible for the deeds of the multinational. Only the multinational is responsible for its deeds. And this multinational has only managers in favour or the board of directors. If we start thinking about this, it is unbelievable that the world has come so far. So far from a situation which could have a balance. The equilibrium of the present world is hard to find. Governments have to reunite in order to keep track with the multinationals. Before these governments are reunited non governmental organisations will have to control the frontier surpassing corporations. The labor movement is well organised in these tasks, but according to me not enough to fight the multinationals. Structural changes are needed and the equal representation of men, earth and capital within the organisation and society are the only real and sensible solution.

2.2.   Inside the organisation.

Inside the corporation the labor is organised in what they call unions. These unions have very often a considerable power within the company. In the United States as well as in Western Europe the unions are a good counterpart for the capitalistic management of the company. The unions are organised in a overlapping way. This means that labourers of different companies, but in the same line of work belong to the same union. Because of this overlapping the union oversee a larger group of labourers. But also the union can oversee the comparisons among the similar companies.

However the unions are working not from within, but from outside. This puts the labor movement almost always automatically against the capital management. Even if these two representatives would work from within the company. The labourers are as much a part of the company as the capital management. In any case by now it is time to reorganise powers and place men next to capitals management both into the company. Of course the third power should be represented also from within the company.

3.   Who represents nature

At the first sight we are likely to think that nature by itself is an not representative force. We do not know how a tree, air or water can form a voice towards the society. We imagine speaking trees or demanding mountains. And as a result we conclude that it is hopeless to wait for this nature, which is not able to represent itself. This hopelessness has lead to quietly going with what we have done until now. Going on with the growth of capital and humans, which are crushing the unrepresented earth. But what we do not see is that the representation of capital is as complex as the representation of nature. And capital was the first represented power. Capital was even sooner a power as men themselves. And capital could not speak either. There were no shouting factories or marching waste baskets. Only humans are able to represent themselves in a direct method. Nature and capital are on the first sight mute powers. But this is untrue, since there are in this world of which, we basically know so little about, much more ways to communicate. Much more ways then, we as people have accepted are possibilities to communicate.

It is our task as humans to feel the pressures of capital, laborers and nature. Capital we represent very well. Men are also represented and now we need to translate the energy of nature into the world of human beings.

Through the organisation, through the society and through the world, we will lead the energy of nature. We as people have to translate this energy into an understandable language for the people. It is not needed to translate these energies for nature or capital themselves. Only we as people need these translations. In being in the process of translating we will become aware of the need or the earth. In the past we have become aware of the needs of capital, by translating the capital energy into understandable figures. These figures are representing capital factor in the present society. Now it is the humans task to bring nature in for humans understandable way to the society.

By translating the earth's energy, the humans themselves will feel the need to form a front for the earth. The peoples will start understanding the earth's needs. A big group of people will start supporting the earth's needs. They will represent the earth in the organisation, in the society and in the world. The earth will be represented together with the factor labor and the factor capital. The representatives will be the people who feel the closest to the earth. There will be people who feel more close to labor. There will be people who feel more close to capital and there will be people who feel more close to nature.

3.1. <u>What is nature</u>

According to me nature is the same as earth an I sue these reversible. In fact nature is a more extensive comprehension, because it includes not only the land surface of the world, as the earth does, but in addition all the entities composing the physical universe. The earth, the nature I call the unmovable since I see these as the untouched. It is the material untouched and not moved by men. It is the world as we knew it on the moment men started adjusting it for its own use. Nature is everything before men has used his intellect to adjust. Nature is the primitive form of capital, since capital is the intellect form of nature. Men was and is the accelerator of the reformation from nature to capital. Nature is the instinct, while capital is the intellect. Intellect is taking too much space for itself and the instinct of mother nature is threatened to go under.

We have to look towards nature as that what is given to us. That what was available before men was around. And with me, I mean the intellect men. The humans who started to adjust the earth. The humans who started working with the nature. People started using the water for cleaning. People started using the soil for building and people started using the air as a place for pollution. All these adjustments had no negative affects on the earth until there was too much of everything. Nature had no capacity anymore to absorb. Nature became more a place to get then a place to live within. Nature was always meant as a safe harbour for people. but the people abused nature and did this by taking too much. Nature has become the place to take and to get. It is not seen as a respected partner anymore. We take and we dump. We used, we reused and we abused.

Now nature will become a power, an energetic power, because it is driven in a corner. It can only escape out of the greedy hands from capital by using its force and showing its strength. Capital was always a much smaller force then nature and therefore never had any problems with becoming bigger. In this vacuum capital was absorbed, this capital was created by reforming nature. More and more nature was needed to reform into capital to fill the vacuum. With the transfer of this energy capital became more powerful, because it became more. Nature became lesser and capital more. It started uneven, therefore capital has gained so much force, now it is again uneven and powers will change again. When powers are changing everything changes, the world will go upside down. We will organise nature, labor and capital in n equal way in balanced society. This option will form in the coming society the least drastic change and therefore the best and easiest change for the society we are familiar with. Capital will have to be reformed back into nature. Reformed capital will be a forceful nature in the coming society.

3.1.1. Earth, water and air.

A simple way to divide nature, which as we have seen, are the entities composing the physical universe. These physical entities are earth, water and ir, but also the animals, plants, trees and human beings. This is a certain division in which nature is parted in solid masses, liquid masses, volatile masses and living masses. It are these masses which are used by the humans to convert them into capital. The adaptable goods. These goods we call the capital factor of existence. All our industry is based on the mining of resources, transporting of these resources and adjusting these resources to usage of the people.

The people themselves in this process are the labourers and therefore the servants of the produced goods. I call them the accelerator in between the factor nature and the factor capital. People in my study are mainly mentioned as men who not mention people as living human beings, just as working labourers. This because my study starts with the three production factors based on the economic studies. In these economic studies people are divided into two groups, consumers and producers. I talk mainly about the producing capacity of the people. Very clear since my starting point is the saving of the earth. It is the industriousness of people which are destroying the earth and not the fact that these same people need to live and consume. In the end it is of course the same discussion£. What I want to tell in this paragraph is that people, in their natural habitat, are also a vital part of nature.

Nature started with liquids, solids and volatiles, but nature went on with animals and people. The part were the earth started to feel the beginning of the end was when men became intellectual. to be consequent in this study I have to emphasise on the consuming capacity of the human being, which is in fact the natural part of the being, humans would be a part of nature. But in my study humans are called labor and as such they are an opposing power of nature. So to make things clear, I do not deny humans of being a port of nature, because they are a part of nature. But I call humans intellectual creatures (animals) who use their intellect to produce goods, and by doing so they destroy nature instead of being a part of nature. The nature, we humans, have to protect by representing it, is existing out of earth, water and air in a direct sense. In addition nature exists out of animals, plants, tees and not intellectual human beings. We as intellectuals are not a part of nature and as such an opponent of nature. Therefore we have the intellectual responsibility to protect nature by representing nature in its fight for survival. The earth, water and air have not other way of representation in order to protect themselves in a human way.

3.1.2.   The animals and greenery.

Within the factor of existence, nature, we have seen that next to earth, water and air, which we will call the primary nature. We also have the so called secondary nature, which we will call the animals, plants, greenery and the not intellectual human beings. In reality of course there are no not intellectual beings, but I see it as essential to make this difference.

The differences;   1. The intellectual people are the producing people.
2. The not intellectual people are the consuming people.

Because I see this difference in between, not intellectual and intellectual people, as the difference which parts producing and consuming people. In which the intellectual people are the producing people. The not intellectual people are the consuming people. This difference for my thesis is essential, because the pure consuming people are within the group of animals, which are a part of nature. The producing group of people are the labourers of the world, and as such the opposing power of nature. So it is important that we make the difference, but in the present history there is no such thing as a not intellectual human being.

In short:
```
1. Nature,     A. primary nature:
                    - earth.
                    - water.
                    - air.
               B. secondary nature:
                    - plants.
                    - trees.
                    - animals.
                    - not intellectual human beings, consuming
                      people.
2. Labor,      A. intellectual human beings, producing people;
                    - managing people.
                    - working people.
3. Capital,    A. available capital.
               B. working capital.
               C. used capital/
```

This paragraph talks about the secondary nature. The most striking difference in between the primary and secondary nature is that the latter can vanish by dying. The former can lonely become different in substance, because the primary nature is not a living substance. And what does not live can not die. It is when the secondary nature is dying that the capital and labor factor clearly become aware of lack of respect towards the factor nature. Where with primary nature, to become aware of a different substance, as a result of neglecting nature, is more difficult to notice. This happens in the primary nature and to see this as an actual danger for whole. Therefore few people mention the dangers for the primary nature, but always mention the dangers for the secondary nature.

The actual dangers for the primary nature are basically very difficult t oversee and to study. Because there is too little known about the very often, long time away from now, results of the present neglecting of nature. The results of neglecting the secondary nature are immediate known. If we kill a deer by car, the result, which shows us the immediate destruction, is obvious. If we produce too much substances which are causing acid rain, we are immediate confronted with nearby dying trees. If the industry is wasting too much chemicals into a lake, the fish in this lake will come to the surface of the water and nature will clearly be harmed. Men and capital can not harm nature, and certainly not obviously the secondary nature, without being punished for their killing deeds.

The greenery and animals take care of each other in filling each others needs. If people want to go on living the way they are used living, then we will have to take care of the greenery and animals. These animals and greenery are a part of nature and therefore nature needs recognition, representation and an equal vote in the future society and future organisation. Nature as an independent power within the society. People will have to come up for this factor nature. And the people will do so.

3.1.3. Nature in today's world.

In the history of the earth nature was always a big self evident energy. In the recent history, in which I mean the last century, since the industrial revolution, nature has become a shrimping power. The intellect of men, the industriousness of capital have forced nature in a position of may limitations. Nature in today's world is a suppressed power, which has to be protected and respected. If we mention today's world we have to mention the basic difference, there are in the today's world. We have to distinguish the three parts of the world, which are singled out by economic reasons.
These are; 1.   the industrial countries.
2.   the poor countries.
3.   the rapidly industrialising countries.

Nature in the industrial counties is respected. It is recognised and the people in these industrial countries are aware of the problems, which are endangering the earth. But at the same time it are the industrialised countries, which are the most polluting of all countries and the most harmful to nature of all countries. The industrialised countries, which are also called the 24 countries of the Organisation for Economic Co-operation (OECD), were in 1989 responsible for 40 percent of global sulphur oxides emissions and 54 percent of nitrogen oxides emissions. These two oxides are the primary sources of acid rain. Also they generated 68 percent of the world's industrial waste as measured by weight. They accounted for 38 percent of the global potential warming impact on the atmosphere from emissions of greenhouse gases. Although the combined population of the industrialised countries was only 849 million or 16 percent of the world's population. So respected or not, nature has a much harder time in the industrialised countries as in the rest of the world. The figures are from the world resources 1992-93, published by World Resources Institute.

Nature in the poor countries, which are the countries identified by the world bank as low income countries. These low income countries have an average annual per capita gross national product (GNP) of less than $ 580,- in 1989. Forty one countries are meeting this criterion. If we use other criteria, following the United Nations Development Program (UNDP) were quality of life is more important than quantity in life, we see that even more countries, sixty three, are released as poor countries. The UNDP looks for example more towards longevity and literacy. In these poverty stricken countries it is mostly the population growth rate which endangers the factor nature all over the world. As a result of this overpopulation the poverty is difficult to be halted. And poverty and environment are intertwined problems, which endanger nature. On the other hand, in the industrialisation countries, it is true that a higher level of living will ask even more from the factor nature. In a way the poverty in the poor countries is better than a higher standard of living, as we know this in the industrialised countries. However the solution can only be found in the limitation of the growth in especially the poor countries. When this limitation is reached we can bring better levels of quality living to these poor countries. With this better quality living the people can develop better skills to threat the earth.

Nature in the rapidly industrialising countries, these are the countries which are positioned in between the industrialised countries and the poor countries. As example Taiwan, Singapore, Hong Kong and South Korea. These countries are on one hand countries with an enormous fast growing industry. It is essential for these rapidly industrialising countries that they start with a nature responsible industry. Next to this nature responsible industry they need to divide their profits from this industry equally among their inhabitants. They have the greatest challenge, because they have no industrial history to rely on and n material and intellectual strong people to fall back on. Basically it are the countries which are developed in a way the whole world would have liked to see all developing countries develop. But nature, in these countries, has the most difficult place, because capital has taken a very important place. Capital is it what made these countries more equal with the leading industrialised countries. Not nature, which is mostly seen ass a limiting factor in their competition with the leading countries. Nature in these countries is not represented because of need, and not because of a incapability of funds.

Nature in today's world has to be represented in the whole world and not only within a certain field. Nature should also be protected in the right order, first in each others own country and only then we should look to our neighbours deeds. We and everybody for themselves should start with the representation of nature in our own society.

3.1.4.   The trinity as saviour.

Nature together with labor and capital will form a platform in which the society and future organisation will be run. These three powers together will become a vast unit, and we will call them together the trinity. This trinity by itself will form a stronghold of unified energy, of which no force can win.

The trinity itself will defend capital.
The trinity itself will defend labor.
The trinity itself will defend nature.

All people will respect this trinity. All factor of existence will respect this trinity. The trinity will not be formed by one organisation, but will be formed in every possible organisation again. These trinities which will lead the societies will become into power because of democratic forces.

It will be the people's wishes that these trinities will from the respected power. Every person will bring out three votes, one for labor, one for nature and one for capital. The trinity will save the earth, because it will represent the hart of the environment.

The way the world is organised now, is not from within, but from one side, very often outside. We should understand the true meaning of the comprehension environment, which is the whole universe. Everything in our universe should be involved. As the centre of the balanced, environmental, society the trinity as its hart will be the saviour of the world.

3.2.   Who will defend nature

Nature itself is showing us many acts of resistance against the crushing power of capital and in a lesser way labor. however this study starts from a point where we will assume responsibility from the people. This responsibility shows us our will to endure; the endurance on its turn shows us our will to go on the way we are now used to it. We want to go on with our lives the way we now know it. The way we are now used living on earth. We people will find a human friendly way to escape the resistance of nature, by representing nature ourselves. So the question, who will defend nature remains and we mean; which people will defend the factor nature?

This question has to be asked from every person. This question is an individual task. Every person has to ask him or herself, what is the role nature plays in my life? We have to ask ourselves, what importance does nature has in our individual lives. But we also we have to ask, what is the role of capital in our life and what is the role of labor in our life. And for each person different priorities will play parts. Since the world is always changing and following evolution, also these questions will evolve according to the time and history. When people will bring the factor nature on a higher level in their personal emotions, this will be an answer on an outburst of natural energy. Or a reaction of people on a sign the earth, nature has given. Indirect it is the earth who will represent itself through the people. The people who become aware of the needs of the earth.

What is the role of nature in our life? For example. If we make a child, it is apparent that this is an act out of nature, it is a natural act. At the same time this child will bring us security for the future. This security know its base in the factor capital. Security is a pure capitalistic item, it has nothing to do with nature or labor. What I want to show is that a natural act can have capital consequences, because first the parents have to labor for the child and later the child has to labor for the parents. No act in life is an act by itself. No reaction in life an act by itself. Always the three factors of existence are involved, the factor nature, the factor labor and the factor capital. So we see the role of nature is as important to life as the role of capital and as the role of labor. The role of nature can not be seen apart. It has to be seen in the trinity, which will represent the three powers and rule the society. Therefore people will always defend nature as well as labor and capital. The original question who will defend nature? Will be answered in the following paragraphs were we will see that the people who now represent capital and labor will eventually defend nature.

3.1.1. The people who defended capital.

The people in general will defend nature, so among these there will be the people who are now calling themselves environmentalists, capitalists or labourers. In this chapter we will see that capital representatives will defend nature. First we have to ask who are these capital representatives? Probably the people who are possessing the most capital, or are possessing the most material. These people normally function in organisations, in societies and corporations as managers. Managers are in fact labourers, but it is in these functions they have the most control over their capital investments.

The capital managers we will call them. These capital managers will go out and represent the earth. Slowly they will see that capital is crushing nature and slowly their initial capital interests will go over into nature interests. Their interests will gradually go over together with the evolution, which finds its way into the whole society. These capital managers will find themselves in a place where their initial duty is to defend and protect capitalism, but because the natural pressure of nature they will see themselves protecting and defending the factor nature.

3.1.2. The people who defended labor.

As in the former paragraph people who are normally defending an opposing power will now defend the power nature. In this paragraph we see that the labourers will defend nature in the near future.

These people we call just labourers, and in defining them, we accept two matters,
1. they are involved in actual labor,
2. they represent the power labor in the society.

Almost everyone is one way or an other involved in doing labor. In the former paragraph we have seen that the capital managers are in fact only labourer. The people who represent nature, the environmentalist, will also be involved in doing labor. They will work for a fee on an hourly base in some kind of organisation. In the former two chapters we have also seen that the labor representatives are already very often involved in the representation of nature.

This representation of nature by third forces is mostly to thank to the vacuum which was created by the lack of nature in the whole.

Labor has done already a lot for nature. Now they will go on in defending their opposing power in the trinity. Because a big part of the people who originally defended labor will feel themselves more in common with the cause of nature.

3.1.3.   Nature itself will accomplish.

All these people, capitalists and labourers, even environmentalists only start defending nature because nature started defending itself. Nature is the direct responsible power for its own cause. The people who will respond in a humanly way to the cry of nature are the indirect representatives. But in a direct sense. It is only the factor of existence nature of earth which is responsible for its defence.

The possibilities for nature to show its pain. Or to show its needed space to survive, are numerous. But we as human beings are not capable in noticing all these reactions nature shows to the world. Although we are aware of certain reactions.

For example;   1. The phenomena, the dying of living creatures.
                    2. The changing in substance of gasses, liquids and solids.

Of both we as people can not be sure if it is bad or good, negative of positive for the worlds existence. The worlds existence is the crucial question for the environmental problem. The environment, the world in a whole, the existence in a whole the way we human are known with it. I call the three powers, labor, capital and nature, for this reason also the three factors of existence. I try to proof that only this division of energy is a possibility, which we can use in the division or organisational power.

But to go back to the two, according to me, reactions of nature to the crushing actions of capital and labor.

The alterations of nature;   1. Dying of living creatures, people, animals and plants.
2. Altering of liquids, solids and gasses.

The people have lived millions of years with these vast possibilities of existence. Now, when this natural existing vastness is disappearing the people get scarred and will react by defending nature instead of the other two factors of existence labor and capital. The earth is defending itself by alteration of its existence. People will not comprehend the earth's alterations and become frightened. They will make a front for the earth and it will be the unasked indirect defence of nature itself. Indirect, because not nature itself will defend, but the people will defend in nature's name.

3.1.4.   The trinity as the fourth unit will defend.

When the three powers labor, capital and earth will have formed a vast unit, in which they can perform a unified power, a fourth power will exist. This fourth power we will call the trinity and this trinity will defend the three separate powers. So the power will be defended by the trinity. This trinity will of course also defend the powers labor and capital. I call this the fourth power. In fact it is, and should be the first, last and only power.

In order to clarify, the defenders of;
1. Nature and earth are naturalists of earth people.
2. Capital are capitalists.
3. Labor are labourers.
4. Trinity and environment are environmentalists.

In order to realise the trinity, e will have to vote in a democratic manner, for the three separate powers. However according to me we should build in a security, that the representation should be equal. However it is also my opinion that this equal representation should be reached in a democratic harmony. If for example nature can not force its need for space within the human representatives, the trinity will be unequal divided. Nature in this case will be lesser represented than labor and capital. At the end of the total process of alterations towards the trinity we need an equal process of alterations towards the trinity we need an equal quantity of votes for the three powers. Every person will have three votes to bring out. One for nature, one for labor and one for capital. In voting in a manner like this every factor ill be assured of an equal quantity of votes. But these representatives of factors can be moderate or extreme. The moderation or extremity will ensure a fair balance in between the fusion of the powers. The fusion of factors. The fusion of powers. The trinity of the future.

But alterations of these extent which will lead to this ultimate fusion, will take a long time. On the other hand time will heal everything. The only question with a statement like this, what will change when the time is healing? Slowly the fusion or trinity will take over the power of the three. And who knows after this, when only the one unit exist, the trinity, there will come a time where a new unknown power will come along again. And maybe this new binary will lead to a new fusion. But that is for much later living creatures.

Back to this trinity, which will have the energy from within to convince the responsible organisations and societies. Not anymore with force from above or against, capital and labor will have to be convinced of the rights of nature. From within, and with respect nature will speak as an equal power. It can and will be the only possible solution for this enormous injustice done towards the earth. The trinity will defend.

3.2.   How long before the world will see

Before the world, the people will see that the factor nature needs to be helped. There still is enough water to drink. There still is enough earth to live on. There still are enough resources to use for the production of capital goods. There still is enough air to breathe. So in fact where do we worry about? If we are smart enough to look in the future, we will know that with the present growth rate of the population and the present decrease of needed air, water and solids, there will com a shortage of these natural goods. At the summit in Rio, June 1992, we talked about sustainable development. In other words we need to sustain the development or we have to comprehend the growth within controllable limits. This statement tells us that we have seen the necessity already. We know that the situation is becoming precarious. So the world is in a position to see.

However if the world is actually seeing and understanding, that is very much still the question. The catholic church, heading millions and millions of faithful people, is still promoting to have children. The capitalistic community still sees only one, criterion or standard to measure their rate of competition. This criterion is the growth of the gross natural product. And these criteria are always mentioned in quantity and not quality. The ridiculous fact that nations are using this kind of figures as nationalistic competing comparisons, while in other parts of the world people are dying from hunger, remains an unbelievable issue. But worse things are happening. The world does not understand that the competition should not be measured by capital growth, but in the growth of nature, or the growth of labor.

What there is too little we should encourage. What there is too much we should discourage. Capital goods we have so much that we have to dump them into refuse heaps. The essence of a refuse heap for example is a direct attack on nature. Because there where was once a vastness of nature, now there is a refuse heap or waste concentration. A concentration of abused and not useful capital. So we see from this example alone, that we have a growing shortage of nature, because the capital industry is working harder than ever. And the waste of capital is growing harder than ever.
Nature is attacked twice;
1. nature is taken, to remake it in capital,
2. used capital is dumped on other nature.

It is a never ending cycle. And while it is happening people are warning for the dangers. But the warnings are not heard, and people go on competing in having the most capital goods. People remain greedy and the world does not see, because of incompetence.

1. More disasters.

What are disasters and how do we recognise disasters. And what are the causes for these disasters. Are they just a part of natural evolution or are they a reaction on the abuse of nature by human beings. Are for example the earth quakes in Middle America a reaction on the United States and French military exercises, which are involved in the trials of nuclear bombs. Is the depleting ozone a reaction o the abuse of dangerous gasses. Or another question, is a depleting ozone dangerous for our world. With proving natural actions or reactions, we do not necessarily proof these natural acts are of a dangerous nature for mankind; It remains always a question if we have to take care. Maybe all these natural reaction, and disasters will have a positive affect on the existence of human beings. But to go on as we know the world, we people are life threatened by disasters and as such we will fight them.

People die in Africa because of the draught. Young people die of AIDS because of a incurable virus infection. Industrial workers die because of exposing themselves to unknown materials; People die because they fight for earthly space. Soldiers die because they fight for natural resources. fish die because water is polluted by the industry. Birds die because they find themselves covered with petrol. Elephants die because too many people want too much ivory. The water in Venice is full with an all overwhelming sea weed, which tries to fight the pollution. Trees are being cut down at a rate, it seems impossible to plant them again. Climates are changing. Atmospheres are changing. Soil degradation and deforestation change complete countries. All these should not be necessarily bad, if not the world population would not been tripling in the second half of this century and the first half of the next century.

More disasters we can not handle, however it does not seem to stop. If these disasters are a direct consequence of the capital abuse of nature we can not say with sureness, but we do know that if we as people could live with less, nature would have room too.

2.   What do we need as proof.

More disasters? More people and animals dying? For example in The Netherlands there are three thousand five hundred polluted areas located. These figures are known. Small scale disasters have happened in The Netherlands with polluted soil, but still general opinion seems to be unalarmed. If we as people are not immediate threatened in our own home, or our own lives, we do not seem to realise any dangers. The truth of the matter is that people in general are too shortsighted. If it would come to a referendum, where each person could voice her or his opinion, I will have fear for the factor nature. People are not of a bad nature, but they are raised in a capital world. This world has taught them that to have money in the bank is more important than to have a tree in the garden. Looking to this comparison, we see how difficult a road we have to finish. But at the same moment we can also see the possible simplicity of the problem.

The companies, which the environment movement will be able to reach, will have always the capitalistic answer back. "We have no money". As answer I have, if it is only money, which can solve this complex earth threatening problem, we should be the happiest people in the universe. If the answer of the company would be they could not follow the environmental which, because they did not have the technical capacity, then the problem would be real. Now there answer is only based a shortage of capital. A factory is asked by an environmentalist, if this industry could plant trees around the manufacturing facilities. The industrious direction answers, no because our budget will not allow us to plant these trees. The answer of the environmentalist will be, then next year you just make your budget different. The only result will be a more expensive consumer price.

So the question, what do we need as proof? The answer is only, the proof is so much money on the budget. The evidence that nature has needs becomes clear, when capital sees a price. If capitalists see an amount, a quantity, they are convinced of seriousness. Badly enough, the seriousness of nature can only be proved with a quantitative answer and not a qualitative answer. For one company with one environmental problem we do not need more evidence than this. It will not hurt the capital industry on the long run. The only problem is the near future. The near future, where the industry will be afraid of will be a not following competition. And indeed this will be true, because it will take a long time before the industry in the whole world will have its environmental rules adjusted to each other and to the environment. This is why it will be of utmost importance that the industries will become more international. (More about this in the last paragraphs of chapter 5, government as an equal.)

But if we need the evidence for the destruction of the whole universe and we need to prove this to the whole universe, it will take more than a price on a budget. In Rio, June 1992 the world leaders came together and budgeted an amount of one hundred twenty five billion U.S. dollars each year until the turn of the century. In away this is making a global budget. The difference is that this budget needs the global consent and to bring this consent together will take a long time. The permission of every single person will be needed and has to be given in freedom. It will be this permission of every single person on earth, that will be the proof of the needs of nature and at the same time the solution.

3. Is nature noticeable for people.

The question is not, do we notice trees, animals, mountains or oceans. The question is, do we people respect and notice nature as an equal. Or do we just belief that we can live and use everything we find and discover her on earth, and this without even the least respect for nature. It is easy just using and pretending if the earth would not be a force by itself.

Nature was always and will probably always be the most noticeable power on earth, simply because everything started with nature.

Now people have come in and started creating capital. The involvement of people with the capital factor is so enormous that nature is suffering. It is strange that such a notorious energy can be such a small part of human existence.

Already people are starting to go from cities and metropolitans towards the county. Either temporarily of for a longer time. But mostly people who are living and spending all of their valuable time into big capital concentrations, are finding their way to nature. It is called recreation, and of course heavily influenced by the capital factor. People are transported to and from the recreational centres. They all spend their time in homogeneous rooms, and occupy their time with homogeneous activities. All this is a step in the right direction, since it is a step back to nature. Nature is becoming, strangely enough on the initiative of capital more noticeable for the people.

2. The future of nature in the society

As seen in the above, organised recreation is a form of nature in the society. But next to recreation there are many other places where nature is touching the society. The garden of households and factories. Plants and animals in family housings. Also farms are operating very close to nature, there is what we have called in the first chapter the available capital. The available capital is the biggest source of nature. It is everything untouched by the society. Untouched and touched nature is a difference in this thesis, which will show its importance in the future. from now on I will call touched nature, cultivated nature, and untouched nature, uncultivated nature. The more the world will grow in capital, in labor and hopefully in nature, the more important cultivated nature will become. For example, when forests are deforested people will have to come in and forest these areas again. This will be a form of cultivated nature. To breed animals in a zoo, to plant trees around a factory, or to clean water before it goes back to the natural surface waters, these will all be a part of cultivated nature. We have seen already that cultivated nature will become a major and needed source of nature. In order to enhance nature we will have to use these capitalistic industrious methods. The world will be a part of the greater evolution. Even if we go back to a form of which we want it to be more a part of history than the future, we will have to accept the evolution. This evolution will show us clearly that to go back to this longing history will not be possible. The evolution itself is the reason, the cause, and the proof. The evolution of time will bring us the cultivated nature, even if we want the uncultivated nature. The better of the two will always be the cultivated nature. So in short we have the following forms of nature;

A. Cultivated nature,
    1. primary nature,
        a. used space on earth.
        b. transported resources.
    2. secondary nature,
        c. men bred animals.
        d. cultivated greenery.

B. Uncultivated nature,
    1. primary nature,
        a. not used space on earth.
        b. untouched resources.
    2. secondary nature,
        c. free animals.
        d. uncultivated greenery.

These forms of nature will not change in appearance or quality, but will change in quantity and importance. Compared with capital as we have seen, it is exactly the opposite, which has to happen. Capital needs to become more quality oriented and lesser in quantity. Nature needs to become more in quantity and is as we know it now already of the needed quality. In the coming paragraphs we will see how nature will or has to alter in order to keep the world going. We first look into the corporation, then the religious groups, then the governmental parties and at last we look into the factor nature as it will alter the people themselves. In short nature in the future society will become a part of our lives, which will seem not to be comprehended at this moment.

2.1.   The future of nature in the corporation.

Nature within the corporation is in fact one of the essential factors of production. These three factors are labor, capital and nature. In talking about nature for the corporation we will see that the need of the production has to be questioned. This essential question will be handled in chapter 6 the last 4 paragraphs.

Now we will only talk about nature itself and as such we distinguish within the factor of nature for the corporation four major units;
1. resources
2. energy
3. earth surface

Separately we will deal with these factors of nature. First I want to talk about the resources. The natural resources needed in the corporation will be more expensive. More expensive because they will be more scarce. Apart from being more scarce the resources will have to be as much as possible recycled. In addition the transportation of these resources to the manufacturing unit will have to be made smaller. Now we do not involve transportation very much in the fight against pollution of nature. Never the less it will become a key issue to diminish transportation as much as possible, since this transportation is a major polluter of nature.

Transportation of men and goods will have to be curbed in the future, because transportation is next to being itself a major contributor to pollution, also a major cause of unjust division of wealth.

Also the remainders of the resources will have to be used or reused in the same manufacturing unit or an other manufacturing unit. The resources which will be used will have to have as much as possible a returning capacity. For example trees can be planted again, and as such return in their former capacity.

In short we see that the resources;
1. will become more scarce, more expensive,
2. have to be more recycled,
3. have to be less transported,
4. remainders have to be reused,
5. have to have returning capacity.

Second we talk about the future changes in the use of energy. The above contains as much truth for the resources as for the energy source. This because natural energy are forms of natural resources. In addition to the above future rules for resources it is important that we have to take measures against the usage in a whole. So apart from questioning the use and reason the people will need this energy, we have to simply forbid a usage more than a certain amount. The logic for this lies behind the truth that every person is born with the power of energy to liver her or his life. And in the future world people will have more time. They will have more time because the world will need less industrialism and therefore people need to be less industriousness. So people will have more time and energy to spend on their own. Additional need for energy can therefore always be questioned. In short we can say that everything which seems now as normal can be questioned in the future. Certainly when this can influence our earth in a positive way.

The third way the future of the corporation shall differ from now, regarding nature, will show itself in the need or better available surface of earth each company will be able to use. No reason to say that the space will have to diminish. The space for the winning of resources, the space for production, and the space for used capital. In addition to these harsh but needed directions the available space for capital will have to be used in a more natural way. Or in other words in a more appropriate manner for nature. The corporations will have to deliver after usage these earth surfaces in the exact way they have got it when they started using it. Of course their will always be exemptions, because a complete clean industry will be a very long time from now. In reference to the space on earth the corporation will have to concentrate itself as much as possible.

3.1.2.   Nature as possible goal for the religions.

Religious groups as well as capital groups follow according to me a too narrow path. If capital only looks to the growth and continuation of the very came capital, religious groups only look to the path which follows a certain theory or doctrine. This doctrine does not bring in the needed forms of energy to come to a balanced society. The base of religion sees itself limited to the other human being. Not the other labourer, but the other human being. In regard to mankind religion oversees a more complete field than labor, because it handles with people in general. Not only people as labourers but people as people in the overall society. Never the less in regard to the trinity, religion only handles mankind, while the trinity handles nature, capital and labor. This is more complete picture, since labor handles the producing side of the people. Both the instinct an intellect sides are comprehended into the trinity. In addition the trinity handles capital and the side of nature, which does not comprehend human beings. As a result, the religious organisations could as well as the capital organisations start organising themselves in a balanced manner. This balanced manner, means the fusion in between labor, capital and nature, which forms the trinity. This trinity is in fact a representative of the environment itself. Environment means the world in a whole, the world without anything excluded. This of course should very much be in the line the religious groups are going to work. Since the original doctrine of the religion falls within this fusion, it will not be a proposal without the possibility of success. But since religion for many of us is a part of the untouchable, I will not farther touch it.

3.1.3. Nature as political party.

When labor came into power they did this mainly with the start of a political movement. Capital never really had the need for a political movement, because they were the one already in power. The political parties which were ruling the world in fact did not have the name of capital, but the only way they knew was capital. Very often the religious party formed a political power, which protected capitalism. Religion as we have seen in the former paragraph had its doctrine in the human beings and as such took capital with it as sideline. But as it goes so often, the sideline became the major force. Whatever happened in the past now, labor has its representation into the politics. Nature started with a political movement and is winning some field. The green party it is often called, but for many it has a ring of fringing actions. It is still a political party on the edge of the society. But never the less the only way for the earth movement to force itself between the ruling parties. We have to understand it is not political power we target, but equal representation of nature in every single organisation. Not only political organisations, but the total of worldly organisations.

It can be safely assumed that political power comes before real power. The political power is only a way of counting and measuring according to capital rules the power of the movement. The people have the power, the labourers shouted a century ago. This seemed to be the truth, because non of the three production factors seem to be so close to the votes of the people. For who else is voting than the people themselves. But capital never had any such a real connection with the votes of the people and always through history had more power than labor. Even now a century after the labor movement called the power to the voters. Capital remains a power bloc. Now nature will come in between and form an additional power bloc. It will manifest itself through the political system, but the real power will have little to do with politics. It will be a force from within human instincts. A force which can not be denied. Nature in politics will only be the start of the way to the balanced society.

3.1.4. The future of Nature in between people.

In the above is most of the nature in between people already discussed. Not in a connection with company, government or religion nature comes even closer to the human being. For people themselves are nature if they do not participate in the production process. Or in other words do not use their intellectual capacities. Nature in between people means to conceive a child, this is a pure instinctive character of the human being. But of course there are much more instinctive characters the human being has. for example to feed itself, to protect itself and to produce itself. All these characters can be found and done in a pure natural habitat. We, people do not need the help of laborers or capital goods to live within nature. Never the less we have adopted ourselves so much that the adoption of labor and capital became an essence in our lives. Now these three form of energy are so intertwined in our lives, it seems impossible for us to start an independent life from capital and labor.

But in the future nature will have to become a more important and more independent energy within the people's life. The protection we will have to try to find within the nature. By using natural resources which have a capacity to return. Or by using simply less natural goods. Or by using goods which have as little as possible production need. The feeding of ourselves we also have to try to find within a limited earthly surface. We should try to grow our own food without capital help and with a lot of our own energy. Our own energy, for this is the energy of nature. Nature in between people will be using the energy of nature. All this with rejecting the help of labor and capital. If we people do not start ourselves with seeing the importance of denying the capital and labor factors, it will not be possible to convince the capital managers and labor representatives.

However with this plea for nature I do not deny totally the capital and labor powers. It is the trinity I defend and not one of the three powers which form the trinity. However it has to e seen that it is nature which is crushed under the weight of capital and labor. Therefore nature has to be helped at the cost of capital. In the end it has to be the balanced trinity.